MODERN RUSSIAN POETRY
AN ANTHOLOGY

CHOSEN AND TRANSLATED

BY
BABETTE DEUTSCH
AND
AVRAHM YARMOLINSKY

British Library Cataloguing-in-Publication Data
A catalogue record for this book is available from the
British Library

CONTENTS

Alexander Pushkin

Alexander Sergeyevich Pushkin was born in Moscow, Russia in 1799. Hailing from a family of Russian nobles, he was educated at the prestigious Imperial Lyceum, where he published his first poem at the age of fifteen. After graduating, he became part of the vibrant and intellectual youth culture of the then-capital, St. Petersburg, and published his first long poem, *Rusian and Lyudmila* (1820).

Barely into his twenties, Pushkin was already recognised as a major literary talent. However, in 1820, having became vocally committed to radical social reform, he was exiled from the Russian capital by the ruling Tsar. After observing and actively backing the early stages of the Greek Revolution (1821-1832), Pushkin moved to Chişinău (now Moldova, then part of the Russian Empire). Here, he penned two long Romantic poems which brought him wide and major acclaim: *The Captive of the Caucasus* and *The Fountain of Bakhchisaray*. Over the next few years, forever under the watchful eye of government censors, Pushkin drifted within the Russian Empire. In 1825, while living at his mother's rural estate in Odessa (now Ukraine, then part of the Russian Empire), he penned what has become his most famous play, *Boris Godunov*. However, it took him six years to publish it, and forty years to get it approved by censors and staged.

Between 1825 and 1832, Pushkin's famous novel in verse, *Eugene Onegin,* was serialized. Now a classic of Russian letters, its eponymous protagonist has served as the model for numerous other Russian literary heroes. In 1831, he met another future great of Russian literature, Nikolai Gogol, and helped publicize much of his work. However, just six years later, the notoriously short-tempered Pushkin challenged a man who had been courting his wife to a duel. The encounter left the Russian mortally wounded, and he died two days later, in February of 1837, aged just 37.

Pushkin's legacy is vast; he is now widely considered to be the greatest Russian poet of all time, and the founder of modern Russian literature. His last home is now a much-visited museum in central St. Petersburg.

Acknowledgments

A few of the poems included in this volume have appeared in *The Dial, The Freeman, The Nation*, and *Poetry*. The excerpt from "The Twelve" was taken from *The Twelve*, by Alexander Blok, translated from the Russian by Babette Deutsch and Avrahm Yarmolinsky (New York, Huebsch, 1920).

MODERN RUSSIAN POETRY

AN ANTHOLOGY

FOREWORD

This volume heaps the anthological Pelion upon the Ossa of translation. It aims to present the lyrical poetry of Russia for the last hundred years by a selection of poems translated by the editors. Within the fences thus set up lay a wide foreign field to pick from: the old-fashioned garden overrun by the rank growth of exotic flowers, beautiful weeds outflanking the hothouse plants. The principle of selection was, so far as might be, æsthetic. Poems were chosen less for their representative quality than for their immediate worth and, of course, their ability to stand the test of translation. In view of the pioneer character of this work, however, some concession was made to historical considerations, and, therefore, part of the material included may appear rather jejune and *vieux jeu*. The effort was to give a brief general glimpse of the classic poets and to treat in greater detail the moderns and contemporaries who are, to the translators, as to the readers, more of a living actuality.

The difficulties of selection are obvious. You may add, you may alter the choice how you will, but the sin of omission will cling round it still. In this case the problem was sharpened by the rigors of translation. These were not mere flowers for the plucking. They had to be transplanted into strange soil, which was not hospitable to them all. Translation has been likened to "the wrong side of a Turkey carpet." The question was how best to carry over, unbroken and undiminished, the colors and contours of the right side. We are attached to the idea that we have given as much to the originals as we took from them. Adherence to metrical and rhythmical structure was possible, owing to the essential likeness between the two languages with regard to versification. In matters of imagery and the finer aspects of technique there was also an attempt to be as faithful as the linguistic media allow. But juggling is a fine art, not unworthy of the service of Notre Dame, and the three bright balls of substance, form, and spirit were not always easy to keep in the air at once. What we continually sought was to produce, in the end, a poem.

The personality of each poet is brought out in a note preceding the selection from his work, and the filiation of poetic movements is briefly indicated in the introductory essay.

And finally a word *pro domo nostra*. While it may be difficult to single out each collaborator's part in the work, it is possible, and perhaps interesting, to define the attitude of each. The one, native to Russian literature, brought to the task all the prejudices and privileges of long intimacy. The other, a stranger, saw it with the fresh vision and untaught caprice of a foreigner, making a less practised and a more personal approach. The one was aware, the other persuaded of the gold in the Scythian earth. The two labored together to wrest it, like the one-eyed Arimaspi, from the guardian gryphons.

BABETTE DEUTSCH.

AVRAHM YARMOLINSKY.

New York, June 28, 1921.

INTRODUCTION

Modern Russian literature took its rise in the early nineteenth century. This was, more or less, the Russian counterpart of the Elizabethan Age. Energizing liberal influences were in the air; men's pulses were stirred by the Napoleonic drama; a national self-consciousness came into being; the winds of a new world were blowing from widened horizons. And there was the same coincidence of favorable environment with the accident of genius. Yet if the English Renaissance found its expression in drama, it is notable that nascent Russian literature blossomed in lyricism. England had her Shakespeare, and Russia had her Pushkin,—with a difference.

He is placed in the company of Dante, Shakespeare and Goethe by his compatriots, yet even they admit that he lacks the universal significance of his elder peers. He remains, however, the national poet acknowledged as the first and perhaps the greatest literary artist of his country, a figure upon whom more admiration and scholarship have been lavished than upon any one else. Had he been accessible to the outside world, its current conceptions of the mood and manner of Russian literature would be different. The Byronism with which he began, early gave place to a reconciliation with reality and to a classic sobriety which made Mérimée declare him "An Athenian captive among the Scythians." The intensity of his passionate nature was governed by a sense of measure and harmony. His poetry has that quality of normalcy and health which render it educative, and to the foreigner—uninteresting. The latter may agree with Flaubert that the Russian master is "flat," and to suspect that his is the unexciting art whose motto is *propria communia dicere.*

Pushkin was surrounded by a Pleiad of lyricists, whose work was of a minor order, but was yet distinguished by a measure of originality. Of these the sombre Baratynsky is now perhaps best remembered. In a sense Tyutchev too belonged to this group. A contemporary of Pushkin, he was under his influence. Yet he survived the master by many years, and the more significant part of his unique contribution to Russian poetry was written much later. Of all the classicists, Tyutchev is most likely to find a way to the understanding and sympathy of the outside world. His is a deep and authentic voice. Through his poetry blows the wind of his thought, as a breeze bellies a sail to a certain shape. It is a pantheistic philosophy, instinct with the profound cosmic sympathies of a Chinese sage on his lonely mountain. His universe was the battleground of light and darkness. Both were native to him. He did not dismiss the "ancient chaos" with the facile gesture of tender-minded idealism, but rather saw in it the dark face of God.

The mantle of Pushkin fell, not upon Tyutchev, who wrote for posterity, but rather upon Lermontov. He was an ego-centric creature, with a romantic nostalgia for the supersensuous. His lyricism is informed with a graceful demonism and a proud pessimism which naturally endear him to a youthful audience.

Lermontov revolted not against the Czar of all the Russias, but against the God of heaven and earth. Yet the growing civic bias made it possible to put a social interpretation upon the disquietude which pervades his work. Thus the forensic Nekrasov, who in the next generation voiced the civic conscience of an epoch of reform, is considered to have issued from Lermontov. Nekrasov's troubled and uneven verse dwelt with the miseries of the peasant and the proletarian. It celebrated the cause of the masses, and made itself the vehicle for the *peccavi* of the gentry, aware of its outstanding debt to the people. The age was also glad to give laurels to the folk-poets, such as Koltzov and Nikitin.

The sixties and seventies—the period in which Nekrasov flourished—harnessed the literary Niagara to political action. The age felt that life is real, life is earnest, and that art is not its goal. The permanent abolition of serfdom was coincident with the temporary abolition of æsthetics. The very existence of a socially indifferent poetry was called into question. In this unfriendly atmosphere a group of poets nevertheless carried on the Pushkin tradition of self-sufficient lyricism. Maikov, Foeth, Alexey Tolstoy and, to a certain extent, Polonsky, all deriving from the idealism of the forties, stand out unrelated to the period in which they wrote. These shared with the French Parnassians an allegiance to the dogma of art for art's sake, and Maikov approached their plasticity and impassivity. Æsthetes are inimical to revolution, not because they love justice less, but because they love beauty more. What defined the isolation of these poets was the fact that they belonged to the conservative camp.

Foeth developed a great lyrical activity toward the close of his life, in the eighties. Those were years of social stagnation and prolific, pale poetry. It was only in the next decade, when the Yellow Book was blooming on London bookstalls and the sunflowers on London lapels, that the first signs of a literary, and primarily lyric revival showed themselves in Russia. It was preceded by proclamations, somewhat like a king who is not too sure of his welcome. The vanguard of theorists included Volynsky, Minsky and Merezhkovsky. Here, reversing the natural order, poetics came before poetry. The champions of modernism revolted against the traditional subservience of literature to social progress. They asserted the autonomy and primacy of art, and offered the milk of mysticism to the soul starved on positivist fare. Above all they preached an individualism, whose watchword was *Fais ce que tu voldras*, and which took to its heart Stirner's anarchy and Nietzsche's a-moralism.

Balmont, Brusov and Sologub were the leading poets who initiated the practice of what Minsky and Merezhkovsky had been preaching, and who founded a school, in the loose sense of the term. This was the symbolist, or as some prefer to call it, neo-romantic school. They were clearly inspired by foreign models, and many declared the whole new poetry a warmed-over French dish. Yet the spontaneous and indigenous character of the movement is now beyond question, its studied eccentricity notwithstanding. It was only for a short time that it showed the earmarks of western *décadence*, although its detractors persisted in the term. Anti-social prejudice, a toying with satanism, and concentration on sex were but a temporary phase. The decadent aspect of Russian modernism is best exemplified by Sologub, an exasperated solipsist, living in a sick, fantasmal world.

The heterogeneity and complexity of the movement can hardly be exaggerated. Each writer is a law unto himself. Yet all share a fevered intensity and the literary method of symbolism. To the true symbolist the measure of a verse echoes the song the morning stars sing together. He posits a correspondence between sensuous and mystic realities, using imagery as the sign of a remote and transcendent significance. It remained for the following generation thus to develop the religious implications of the theory. As for Balmont, with his fluent spontaneity, and Brusov, in his more slow and solid achievement, they are chiefly concerned with problems of form and with the cult of a beauty founded upon a flight from reality. This holds good for the sinister magic of Sologub in his early work. All three, especially Brusov, are conscious craftsmen, with an authentic musical gift. They have greatly enriched the medium which they employ.

While the symbolist school united the best talents, there were of course poets who remained *extra muros*. The most important of them is Bunin, a lyricist of rare economy and sensitiveness to color. He carries on the classic tradition, remote from the violences and vagaries of his fellows.

A curious incident in the history of Russian symbolism is the career of Alexander Dobrolubov. One of the earliest disciples of the French *décadents*, he ended as a sectarian prophet. He lived in a coffin-shaped room, papered in black, where he sought Baudelaire's "*paradis artificiels*" by consuming opium and smoking hashish, and whence he issued, clad in black even to his eternal gloves, to preach suicide to his fellow-students. He became in the end a holy vagabond, wearing the coarse clothes of the Volga peasant, and leading a large mystic sect. Dobrolubov's evolution is to a certain extent typical of the development of the symbolist movement. This, beginning with a revolt against the tyranny of utilitarian morality, ended with the reassertion of the ineluctable ethos and a deepened mysticism.

Synchronously with the revolution of 1905 a group of younger men within the fold began to transvalue the symbolists' transvaluations, aided and abetted by the older symbolists themselves. Chief among the newcomers were Ivanov, Bely, Blok and Voloshin. They were impatient of the cult of beauty and looked askance at the gambols of the free individual. Their poetry is passionate metaphysics, groping toward religious ultimates. Spiritually deriving from Solovyov and Dostoyevsky, they are engaged with religion and, to a large extent, with the messianic rôle of the Russian people. In Ivanov and professedly in Chulkov, mysticism is wedded to a curious collectivism. Ivanov declares his verse to be the carven crystal cup for the sacred wine of communal religious consciousness. While in France symbolism contented itself with the part of a literary method, in Russia it tended to become a philosophy and even an ethics.

Problems of technique as such are no longer in the foreground. Symbolism is now considered the characteristic of all poetry. Substance is what these sophisticated lyricists are seeking. And so we find them turning to the imperishable gods of Hellas, wandering down exotic vistas, exploring with Gorodetzky the native folklore, embracing with Kuzmin the delights of *stylization*. A doctrinaire fury rides all these poets. They are inveterate preface-writers, and, what is worse, do not leave their prefaces entirely out of their art, forgetting that philosophy, in Symons' words, is the dung which lies at the roots of poetry.

Shortly before the war the symbolist impetus was felt to have spent itself. There was a general dissatisfaction with the spirit which informed it. The poets, says a Russian critic, were tired of plumbing the ultimate depths of the soul, and of daily ascending the Golgotha of mysticism. After the ecstasies came the desire for the ice-water of simplicity. No longer expressing mystery in music, the poets sought the limited, precise, concrete image. This movement manifested itself in the Acmeist secession. Grouped around a publishing firm, known as the Guild of Poets, which has this year been revived, the Acmeists or Adamists, led by Gumilev, Akhmatova and Gorodetzky, attacked symbolism, to celebrate raw reality. Proclaiming the primitive vision of a Gauguin, they insisted on immediate contact with the tangible, visible, audible world. The coterie did not write much more than its manifesto, though its method may be discovered in the work of the later "imazhinist" (imagist) group, of which Yesenin and Marienhof are representative members. These build their poetics upon the concept of the autonomous image, regarded as the end of all poetry. One of their number has recently declared that a poem must be not an organized entity, but rather a succession of such self-sufficient images, moving as in dreams.

A sensational career awaited the other post-symbolist development, futurism. It originated with the cubo-futurists in Moscow in 1911 and a year later the Petrograd ego-futurists issued their manifesto. The difference between them was rather like that between Tweedledum and Tweedledee, the one hitting everything it could see—when it got really excited, the other hitting everything within reach, whether it could see it or not. They hit out less to *épater le bourgeois* than professedly to discard all the canons of art and to destroy toothless Ratio. Their proclaimed desire was to raze the past and build the present on nothing. Their poetics provide for a language consisting of elements having an audible and a visual, but no intellectual value. This is merely an ideal which, luckily for the rest of us, their poetry does not always achieve.

"Let us gorge ourselves with the void," says one of them. The poetic gift can thrive even on this futile diet. Through their cacophony is sometimes heard the shrill and raucous voice of a machine-made age, their distorted language occasionally mirrors a time which is out of joint, and their violently eccentric imagery wrests new meanings from old commonplaces, as in Mayakovsky's line: "A bald lantern voluptuously takes off the blue stocking from the street." Naturally, they resist translation, except in the case of Severyanin, the early leader of the Petrograd group, whose work is, however, not typical.

Futurism showed no great vitality, and would probably have

shared the fate of a fashion, were it not for the revolution. Its unabashed iconoclasm, its plebeian exuberance, may account for its recent vogue. Its mannerisms are noticeable in the work of men who do not strictly adhere to the coterie, such as Oreshin and Marienhof.

It is worth noting that the literature of the revolution is chiefly verse. The surviving representatives of classicism and symbolism, with the possible exception of Andrey Bely, continue their work without developing it. In addition to them and to the irruption of the futurists, there are the peasant poets, headed by Kluyev, and a large body of workman poets. The revolution has extended the class principle to æsthetics and takes special pains to promote the literary expression of the masses. Yet proletarian verse is by no means a new phenomenon in Russia. From 1908 to 1915 fifty volumes of such verse found their way to publication. The crudity and naïveté of the workmen's poetry produced since the revolution is redeemed by a hard-handed grasp on reality. The return to realism is the promise of a new development in Russian poetry. Like all living things, poetry endures only through change.

ALEXANDER PUSHKIN

(1799-1837)

Alexander Pushkin was born the last year of the eighteenth century. He died at the age of Byron. Within these thirty-seven years he crowded the activity of a great and authentic initiator in literature.

His mother's grandfather was a Negro (or an Arab) who, the story goes, was bought for Peter the Great at Constantinople for a bottle of rum, and who married a German. His father was descended from an ancient Russian family. The poet, inheritor of these curious strains, was educated chiefly by ineffectual French tutors and an old Russian nurse. At eighteen he graduated from an aristocratic school at Tsarskoe Selo, an indifferent scholar, but a writer with a reputation for light and lewd verse. The next three years he spent at the northern capital, where "all the vices dance upon the knees of folly." He was nominally attached to the Foreign Office, but was chiefly sowing his wild oats. By his liberal velleities and merciless epigrams he stung the authorities to the Countercheck Quarrelsome, and the *enfant terrible* was shipped south and subsequently to his own estate. During his not too disagreeable southern exile he divided his time with persistent unfaithfulness between the maids and the Muse. Back in Petersburg, in 1826, he was lionized by the ladies and harassed by the censors. At thirty-two he married a girl nearly half his age, with the face of a madonna and the soul of a brainless coquette. To provide for her needs, the poet worked feverishly, and that she might be received at court, he secured a court appointment. Financial cares and domestic worries soon saddened and aged him. He was destroyed by the aristocratic philistines whose good graces he half-unwillingly sought. An intrigue, involving Pushkin's wife and her brother-in-law, Baron Dantés (D' Anthés), resulted in a duel in which the poet was mortally wounded, at the age of thirty-seven.

Pushkin's share of this volume is no indication of his relative significance in the advance of Russian poetry. He is an overshadowing figure, and, his work is an essential part of Russia's literary endowment. Yet an anthology which is not primarily concerned with historic values, and which is addressed to a foreign audience, can present but a few of his facets to the reluctant light of a sophisticated intelligence.

A NEREID

Among the glaucous waves that kiss gold Tauris' beaches

I saw a Nereid, as dawn flushed heaven's reaches.

I barely dared to breathe, hid in the olive trees,

While the young demigoddess rose above the seas;

Her young, her swan-white breast above the waters lifting,

From her soft hair she wrung the foam in garlands drifting.

"BEHOLD A SOWER WENT FORTH TO SOW"

With freedom's seed the desert sowing,

I walked before the morning star;

From pure and guiltless fingers throwing—

Where slavish plows had left a scar—

The fecund seed, the procreator;

Oh vain and sad disseminator,

I learned then what lost labors are. . . .

Graze if you will, you peaceful nations,

Who never rouse at honor's horn!

Should flocks heed freedom's invocations?

Their part is to be slain or shorn,

Their dower the yoke their sires have worn

Through snug and sheepish generations.

THREE SPRINGS[1]

Three springs in life's unbroken joyless desert

Mysteriously issue from the sands:

The spring of youth, uneven and rebellious,

Bears swift its sparkling stream through sunny lands;

Life's exiles drink the wave of inspiration

That swells the limpid fount of Castaly;

Bur 'tis the deep, cold wellspring of oblivion

That slakes most sweetly thirst and ecstasy.

[1] Tr. by Avrahm Yarmolinsky.

THE PROPHET

I dragged my flesh through desert gloom,

Tormented by the spirit's yearning,

And saw a six-winged Seraph loom

Upon the footpath's barren turning.

And as a dream in slumber lies

So light his finger on my eyes,—

My wizard eyes grew wide and wary:

An eagle's, startled from her eyrie.

He touched my ears, and lo! a sea

Of storming voices burst on me.

I heard the whirling heavens' tremor,

The angels' flight and soaring sweep,

The sea-snakes coiling in the deep,

The sap the vine's green tendrils carry.

And to my lips the Seraph clung

And tore from me my sinful tongue,

My cunning tongue and idle-worded;

The subtle serpent's sting he set

Between my lips—his hand was wet,

His bloody hand my mouth begirded.

And with a sword he cleft my breast

And took the heart with terror turning,

And in my gaping bosom pressed

A coal that throbbed there, black and burning.

Upon the wastes, a lifeless clod,

I lay, and heard the voice of God:

"Arise, oh prophet, watch and hearken,

And with my Will thy soul engird,

Through lands that dim and seas that darken,

Burn thou men's hearts with this, my Word."

VERSES WRITTEN DURING A SLEEPLESS NIGHT

Sleep I cannot find, nor light:

Everywhere is dark and slumber,

Only weary tickings number

The slow hours of the night.

Parca, jabbering, woman-fashion,

Sleeping night, without compassion,

Life, who stirs like rustling mice,

Why encage me in thy vise?

Why the whispering insistence,—

Art thou but the pale persistence

Of a day departed twice?

What black failures dost thou reckon?

Dost thou prophesy or beckon?

I would know whence thou art sprung,

I would study thy dark tongue . . .

WORK

Here is the long-bided hour: the labor of years is accomplished.

Why should this sadness unplumbed secretly weigh on my heart?

Is it, my work being done, I stand like a laborer, useless,

One who hall taken his pay, alien to unwonted tasks?

Is it the work I regret, the silent companion of midnight,

Friend of the golden-haired Dawn, friend of the gods of the hearth?

MADONNA

Not by old masters, rich on crowded walls,

My house I ever sought to ornament,

That gaping guests might marvel while they bent

To connoisseurs with condescending drawls.

Amidst slow labors, far from garish halls,

Before one picture I would fain have spent

Eternity: where the calm canvas thralls

As though the Virgin and our Saviour leant

From regnant clouds, the Glorious and the Wise,

The meek and hallowed, with unearthly eyes,

Beneath the palm of Zion, these alone. . . .

My wish is granted: God has shown thy face

To me; here, my Madonna, thou shalt throne:

Most pure exemplar of the purest grace.

YEVGENY BARATYNSKY

(1800-1844)

"It is a little cup, but it is my own," thus might Baratynsky sum up the small perfection of his art He belonged to Pushkin's school, but was not eclipsed by the master. His *œuvre* consists of one slender volume of lyrics. These are marked by the originality of the discriminating eclectic, by a strong conscience for form, and by the obtruding intellection of a born pessimist.

Like most of the Russian *littérateurs* of the first half of the nineteenth century, with which he was born, Baratynsky belonged to the kept classes. An infringement of the eighth commandment while he was at school (the Corps of Pages) reduced this son of a senator to a mere private. The experience may have accented his gloomy temperament. Aside from this, the outward circumstances of his life, including his marriage, were happy, and therefore have no history. His last years, however, were saddened by the consciousness of estrangement from the rising generation.

PRAYER

King of Heavens! Release

My sick soul to its peace!

For the errors of earth

Send oblivion's dearth;

To thy stern paradise

Give my heart strength to rise.

ALEXEY KOLTZOV

(1809-1842)

Koltzov might best be described as a tame Burns. The adjective applies to the poetry more than to the poet, though even here we find a soberer man. He was a cattle-dealer and the son of a cattle-dealer: a cross between a trader and a cow-puncher. He spent his life in the sordid surroundings of his native town, with the exception of a few visits to the two capitals. There he met the literati of the day, dinnered wi'lairds, and was stared at in fashionable salons. He returned with a swollen head, which caused him a great deal of misery at home. The effect of his intercourse with the intellectuals was seen to be equally lamentable in his attempts at philosophic poetry. His last years were embittered by poverty, neglect, and a tragic love which ended in a lurid disease.

His art maintained his umbilical connection with the people. He carries on the tradition of the Russian folk-song, whether the stuff of his lyrics is the works and days of the peasant, or themes of universal emotional appeal. He uses the free rhythms of the folk-song and, curiously enough, his

31

favorite metre coincides with that of the Sophoclean choruses. Of his one hundred and twenty-four poems, three-fourths have been set to music by some one hundred Russian composers, among whom are Glinka and Rimsky-Korsakoff.

AN OLD MAN'S SONG

I shall saddle a horse,

A swift courser, he,

I shall fly, I shall rush,

As the hawk is keen,

Over fields, over seas,

To a distant land.

I shall overtake there

My young youth again.

I shall make myself spruce

Be a blade again,

I shall make a fine show

For the girls again.

But alas! no road leads

To the past we've left,

And the sun will not rise

For us in the west.

MIKHAIL LERMONTOV

(1814-1841)

Whether or not the semi-legendary Thomas of Erceldoune, who received his poetic gift from the fairies, was Lermontov's ancestor, it is certain that the Russian poet traced his lineage back to George Learmont of Scotland, who settled in Russia in the seventeenth century. His grandchildren claimed that they were descended from that Learmont who fought with Malcolm against Macbeth.

Lermontov's immediate heredity was rather poor. His hysterical mother died in 1817, when he was three years old, and he grew up as the bone of contention between his father and his wealthy, overbearing grandmother. On her estate the spoiled darling received his early education, of the usual imported type. He was extraordinarily precocious in both love and literature. Between 1828 and 1832 he had written 300 lyrics, 15 long narrative poems and 3 dramas. He was little more than a boy when he graduated from a military college at St Petersburg, having previously spent two years at the University of Moscow, and plunged into "a life of poetry, drowned in champagne." His technique as a heart-breaker was only excelled by his power as a poet, and that, in spite of a repellent exterior. Upon Pushkin's death Lermontov's obituary poem brought him rapid fame and exile to the Caucasus. This region was to the poets of Russia what Italy has been to those of England. The romantic glamor of the enchanted land suffused Lermontov's work. One of his flames called him a Prometheus chained to the rocks of the Caucasus, but he was more like a pendulum swinging between them and the *beau monde* of St. Petersburg. He indulged inordinately in the sadism of sarcasm, and was as well hated by the men as he was loved by the women. Spared by the bullets of the mountaineers, Lermontov was killed in a duel with an outraged colleague, only a year older at his death than was John Keats.

Yet this brilliant bully and egotistic rake was, after his own fashion, a knight of the Holy Grail and a poetic genius such as rarely graces any language.

THE ANGEL

Through the heavens of midnight an angel was sped
Who lifted his chant as he fled.
The moon and the clouds and the stars leaned to hear
The song rising holy and clear.

He sang of the spirits, the sinless, the blest,
>   Who softly in Paradise rest.
Of the gardens of God, and of God was his song,
>   Ringing true as a heavenly gong.

He bore a young soul to the dark gates of birth,
>   Toward the travailing, sorrowful earth.
And flying, he sang, and the eager soul heard
>   The deathless, the unuttered Word.

And the years in the world could but sadden and tire
>   The soul filled with wondrous desire.
And vainly the dull songs of earth would have stilled
>   The song wherewith heaven had thrilled.

THE CUP OF LIFE

We drink life's cup with thirsty lips.
Our eyes shut fast to fears;
About the golden rim there drips
Our staining blood, our tears.

But when the last swift hour comes on,

The light long hid is lit,

From startled eyes the band is gone,

We suffer and submit.

It is not our part to possess

The cup that golden gleamed.

We see its shallow emptiness:

We did not drink—we dreamed.

GRATITUDE

For all, I thank Thee, I, the meek remitter:

For passion's secret torments without end,

The kiss of venom, and the tears too bitter,

The vengeful enemy, the slanderous friend,

The spirit's ardor on the desert squandered,

For every lash of life's deceiving thong;

I thank Thee for the wastes where I have wandered:

But heed Thou, that I need not thank Thee long.

FROM "THE DAEMON" (Part I, XV)

On the sightless seas of ether,
Rudderless, without a sail,
Choirs of stars uplift their voices,
Where the mist-waves rise and fail.

Through the hemless fields of heaven
Wander wide and tracelessly
Clouds, unshepherded, unnumbered,
Pale, ephemeral and free.

Hour of parting, hour of meeting,
Neither gladden them, nor fret;
Theirs no yearning toward the future,
Theirs no haunting of regret.

On the grim day of disaster
These remember, worlds away:
Be beyond earth's reach as these are,
And indifferent as they.

CAPTIVE KNIGHT

Silent I sit by the prison's high window,

Where through the bars the blue heavens are breaking.

Flecks in the azure, the free birds are playing;

Watching them fly there, my shamed heart is aching.

But on my sinful lips never a prayer,

Never a song in the praise of my charmer;

All I recall are far fights and old battles,

My heavy sword and my old iron armor.

Now in stone armor I hopelessly languish,

And a stone helmet my hot head encases,

This shield is proof against arrows and sword-play,

And without whip, without spur, my horse races.

Time is my horse, the swift-galloping charger,

And for a visor this bleak prison grating,

Walls of my prison are heavy stone armor;

Shielded by cast-iron doors, I am waiting.

Hurry, oh fast-flying Time, fly more quickly!

In my new armor I faint, I am choking.

I shall alight, with Death holding my stirrup,

Then my cold face from this visor uncloaking.

FYODOR TYUTCHEV

(1803-1873)

Tyutchev was rediscovered by the moderns and hailed as the great fore-runner. They found in his mentality and sensibility, as well as in his technique, elements foreign to classic normalcy, and akin to their own anguished metaphysics and æsthetics. The two hundred short lyrics, which are all the original poetry he has left us, exhibit the organic coherence and ordered beauty which belong to fine lyric art. The originality of his poems consists in that both man's routine passions and nature's passionless routine are sensed in ultimate, cosmic terms.

Tyutchev's career could not be inferred from his poetry. This was the by-product of a long and largely conventional life. He was a sedate bureaucrat in the diplomatic service, a position which kept him in Muenchen, the German Athens, during his best years. He proved the happiness of his marriage to a Bavarian aristocrat by marrying again shortly after her death. When he was on the shady side of fifty his career was seriously injured by a liaison with his daughter's teacher. During the last twenty years of his life he acted as censor, a

41

position for which his political views eminently fitted him. He believed in autocracy, and he prophesied that Orthodox Russia, at the head of the united Slavs, would be the sacred arc riding the waves of the western revolutionary deluge.

TWILIGHT[1]

Soft the dove-hued shadows mingle,

Color fades, sound droops to sleep.

Life and motion melt to darkness

Swaying murmurs far and deep.

But the night moth's languid flitting

Stirs the air invisibly:

Oh, the hour of wordless longing;

I in all, and all in me.

Twilight—tranquil, brooding twilight,

Course through me, serene and smooth;

Quiet, languid, fragrant twilight,

Flood all depths, all sorrows soothe,

Every sense in dark and cooling

Self-forgetfulness immerse,—

Grant that I may taste extinction

In the dreaming universe.

[1] Tr. by Avrahm Yarmolinsky and Cecil Cowdrey.

"AS OCEAN'S STREAM"

As ocean's stream girdles the ball of earth,

From circling seas of dream man's life emerges,

And as night moves in silence up the firth

The secret tide around our mainland surges.

The voice of urgent waters softly sounds;

The magic skiff uplifts white wings of wonder.

The tide swells swiftly and the white sail rounds,

Where the blind waves in shoreless darkness thunder.

And the wide heavens, starred and luminous,

Out of the deep in mystery aspire.

The strange abyss is burning under us;

And we sail onward, and our wake is fire.

SILENTIUM[1]

Be silent, hidden, and conceal

Whate'er you dream, whate'er you feel.

Oh, let your visions rise and die

Within your heart's unfathomed sky,

Like stars that take night's darkened route.

Admire and scan them and be mute.

The heart was born dumb; who can sense

Its tremors, recondite and tense?

And who can hear its silent cry?

A thought when spoken is a lie.

Uncovered springs men will pollute,—

Drink hidden waters, and be mute.

Your art shall inner living be.

The world within your fantasy

A kingdom is that waits its Saul.

The outer din shall still its call,

Day's glare its secret suns confute.

Oh, quaff its singing, and be mute.

[1] Tr. by Avrahm Yarmolinsky.

AUTUMN EVENING

The light of autumn evenings seems a screen,

Some mystery with tender glamor muffling. . . .

The trees in motley, cloaked in eerie sheen,

The scarlet leaves that languid airs are ruffling,

The still and misty azure, vaguely far,

Above the earth that waits her orphan sorrow,

And bitter winds in gusty vagrance are

Forerunners of a bleak, storm-driven morrow.

The woods are waning; withered is the sun;

Earth shows the smile of fading, meekly tender

As the high shyness of a suffering one,

In noble reticence of sad surrender.

JULY 14, AT NIGHT

Not yet cooled, the windless night

Of July shone strangely still.

Earth lay dim, and fitful light
In the skyey, storm-filled height
Trembled over field and hill.

So might lidded eyes unclose,
And between vast lashes burn
Glances flaming and morose,
Over earth's remote repose,
Mute as lightning, swift and stern.

"OH, THOU, MY WIZARD SOUL"

Oh, thou, my wizard soul, oh, heart
That whelming agony immerses,
The threshold of two universes
In cleaving these, tears thee apart.

And so two alien worlds are thine:
Thy day of morbid passionate living,
Thy sleep, vague revelations giving
Of spirits secret and divine.

Then let the tortured bosom beat

With fatal passion and vagary;

The soul is fain, even as Mary,

To cling forever to Christ's feet.

NIKOLAI NEKRASOV

(1821-1877)

Nekrasov's literary career began with a series of prose potboilers, written while he was starving in St. Petersburg. He had come to this city as a boy of seventeen in 1838, to follow the military profession. Against the will of his father, a brute of an *hobereau*, the young man preferred the university to the army, and was forthwith thrown on his own resources. A penniless hack, he became before long a popular poet and the thriving publisher of the two greatest radical monthlies in Russia.

As a child he had heard the bitter songs of the Volga barge-towers. In the capital he had lived with filth and famine. He introduced these elements into his work. Yet though he suffered with the people in his poems, he enjoyed his prosperity, in spite of ethical scruples.

His work is marked by a strong social and civic preoccupation. He declared that this interest interfered with his poetry. As a matter of fact, his "Muse of Vengeance and Wrath" was an uncertain creature. He threw untransmuted into his poetry the raw stuff of satire and feuilleton, of parody and pamphlet. At his best he can move the reader with his stinging pity and his passionate self-scorn. He is perhaps chiefly remembered by his epic: "Who Lives Happily in Russia?", which holds in its vast frame the very essence of the misery and the thwarted vigor of the Russian peasant.

"THE CAPITALS ARE ROCKED WITH THUNDER"

The capitals are rocked with thunder

Of orators in wordy feuds.

But in the depths of Russia, yonder,

An age-old awful silence broods.

Only the wind in wayside willows,

Coming and going, does not cease;

And corn-stalks touch in curving billows

The earth that cherishes and pillows,

Through endless fields of changeless peace.

"MY POEMS! WITNESSES OF UNAVAILING"

My poems! Witnesses of unavailing

Tears for the sad earth shed!

Born in the moment when the soul is failing,

 And by the storm-winds bred;

Against men's hearts you beat with wistful wailing

 Like waves on cliffs as dead.

THE SALT SONG

(From "Who Can Live Happily in Russia?")

God's will be done!

No food he'll try,

The youngest son—

Look, he will die.

A crust I got,

Another bit—

He touched it not:

"Put salt on it!"

Of salt no shred,

No pinch I see!

"Take flour, instead,"

God whispered me.

Two bites, or one—

His mouth he pouts,

The little son.

"More salt!" he shouts.

The bit appears

Again all floured,

And wet with tears

It was devoured.

The mother said

She'd saved her dear. . . .

Salt was the bread—

How salt the tear!

ALEXEY K. TOLSTOY

(1817-1875)

Alexey Tolstoy was a playmate of Alexander II and sat on the knees of Goethe. Like Ruskin, he made a cult of beauty, humanitarianism and Italy. In this second fatherland of his, he began to travel early in life. This courtier-æsthete was a mystic, with a leaning toward the occult. He regarded the doctrine of equality as "the foolish invention of 1793," and was wholly out of sympathy with the materialistic iconoclasts of his time. Yet he was too much of an aristocrat not to despise despotism.

His literary activity began in his middle years. His romantic interest in the Russian past produced a novel and a dramatic trilogy. The past is also the playground of Tolstoy's poetry. This frequently degenerates into pastiche. Nevertheless he was a major poet among the minor poets, at his best achieving a neat and graceful lyricism. His technique is unusual in Russian poetry for its prosodic freedom.

MY LITTLE ALMOND TREE

My little almond tree

Is gay with gleaming bloom,

My heart unwillingly

Puts forth its buds of gloom.

The bloom will leave the tree,

The fruit, unbidden, grow.

And the green boughs will be

By bitter loads brought low.

"A WELL, AND THE CHERRY TREES SWAYING"

A well, and the cherry trees swaying

Where bare girlish feet trod the fruit;

Nearby the damp imprint betraying

The stamp of a heavy nailed boot.

Stilled now is the place of their meeting,

But nothing the silence avails:

In my brain passion's echo repeating

Their whispers—the splash of the pails.

"OH, THE RICKS"

Oh, the ricks, the ricks,

In the meadows lying,

The eye cannot count

You, for all its trying.

Oh, the ricks, the ricks,

In the green morasses,

What do you guard:

You heaped, heavy masses?

Pray, behold us, good sir:

We were once bright flowers;

But the sharp scythe falls

And the whole field cowers.

We were littered here,

All mown down and shattered,

On the meadowland

From each other scattered.

We have no defense:
Evil guests come clawing—
And upon our crests
Perch the black crows, cawing.

On our heads they perch,
The starred heavens dimming.
Here the jackdaws flock,
Their foul hutches trimming.

Oh, thou eagle, hail!
Our far father flying,
Oh, thou fire-eyed, come,
Our bleak foes defying.

Oh, thou eagle, hail!
Lo, our groans grow stronger.
Let the evil crows
Blacken us no longer.

Oh, avenge us swift,

From the heavens swooping;
Punish their vile pride
Till their wings fall drooping:

Till the feathers fly;
Come, a bolt of thunder,
That the steppe's wild wind
Tear them all asunder.

APOLLON MAIKOV

(1821-1897)

Born of a mother with a literary leaning and an aristocratic father, who gave up the military career for that of a painter, Maikov himself was a sculptor who lost his way in literature. He studied painting in his youth, and indeed his poems show a clear sense of line and color, but his best work is marked by a truly sculptural quality. He received a thorough classical education and in his early work he imitated the Greek and Roman masters. Generally speaking, he yields all too easily to the indirections of erudition and to the Protean pleasures of promiscuous translation. It is in the classical genre that he achieves a small excellence. His finest craftsmanship is shown in enamels and cameos, and in clay medallions, but he has neither the paganism of Gautier nor the sensitive sophistication of Régnier. Maikov's is a baptized Pan and a feigning Bacchus.

His later work was dominated by a nationalistic bias which opposed the chosen Russian people to "the rotten West." A typical æsthete, Maikov found himself in the conservative camp. For nearly half a century he served his monarch as a censor. The antinomy of east and west, of Christianity and paganism, viewed with a cold objectivity, superseded his interest in the antique world. This is the pivotal idea of his greatest narrative poem, the tragedy of "The Two Worlds."

ART

Idly I cut me a reed by the shore where the sea heaves and thunders,—

Dumb and forgotten it lay in my simple, my wind-beaten cabin.

Once an old traveler passed who remained for the night in our dwelling,—

(Foreign his dress and his tongue, an old man who was strange to our region.)

Seeing the reed, he retrieved it, and lopping and piercing the nodules,

Sweetly his lips he applied to the holes that he fashioned: responding,

Swiftly the reed-voice awoke, till the noise of the sea breathed within it;

Thus would wild Zephyros blow, were he suddenly ruffling

the waters,

Fingering lightly the reed-stems and flooding the banks with the sea-sound.

"UPON THIS WILD HEADLAND"

Upon this wild headland, crowned meanly with indigent rushes

And withering bush and the pitiful green of the pine-trees,

The aged Meniskos, a sorrowful fisherman laid

His son who had perished. His youth the sea, motherwise, nurtured.

That sea whose wide lap took him back, who resistlessly bore him

In death, and who carefully carried the young body shoreward.

Then mourning Meniskos went forth, and beneath the great willow

He dug him a grave, a plain stone he set for a mark on the cliff-side,

And hung overhead a coarse net he had woven of willow,—

A fisherman's wreath to be poverty's bitter memento.

SUMMER RAIN

"Golden rain! Golden rain! out of the sky!"

Children sing out and run after the rain.

"Quiet, my children, we'll reap it again,

Only we'll gather the gold in the grain—

In the full granaries fragrant with rye."

AFANASY SHENSHIN-FOETH

(1820-1892)

It is said that Foeth, like the nightingale, sang only at dawn and at sunset. Between 1840 and 1856 he published three volumes of poetry. The following two decades he devoted to the pleasures and profits of a gentleman farmer. He waxed fat and prosperous. His famous apple-cakes were sent to no less a friend than Alexander III. On the road to the ripe old age of three score and ten, the poet superseded the *pomeshchik* and paid court to the Muse with four volumes of verse.

Although an admirer and translator of Schopenhauer, Foeth enjoyed the distinction of being one of the few men who were actually happy in Russia. He had an Horatian serenity, and the æsthete's indifference to society's ills. These elements in his character alone are reflected in his poetry, which is written in major, yet has withal the ethereal, insubstantial quality of dream experience. His lyrics are invested with a rarefied sensuousness, a keen feeling for life's cosmic context, and a dominating interest in melody. Tchaikovsky, who set many of his poems to music, likened Foeth to Beethoven.

"WHISPERS. TIMID BREATHING"

Whispers. Timid breathing. Trilling
   Of a nightingale.
Heaving silver waters rilling
   In the quiet vale.

Night's dim light and shadows dreaming
   Through the haze of space.
Moods like faery lanterns gleaming
   On the dearest face.

Smoky clouds show roses sleeping,
   Amber lights and fawn.
Kisses soft, and softer weeping.
   And the dawn, the dawn!

THE AERIAL CITY

At daybreak there spread through the heavens
Pale clouds like a turreted town:
The cupolas golden, fantastic,

White roofs and white walls shining down.

This citadel is my white city,

My city familiar and dear,

Above the dark earth as it slumbers,

Upon the pink sky builded clear.

And all that aerial city

Sails northward, sails softly, sails high;

And there on the height, some one beckons,—

But proffers no pinions to fly.

SWALLOWS

Calm Nature's idle spy, I follow

In joy her pathways; free and fond,

I watch the arrow-winged swift swallow

Who curves above the dusking pond.

It dashes forward, lightly skimming

The glassy surface, half in fear

Of alien clutching waters—dimming

The lightning wings before they veer.

And once again the same quick daring,

And once again the same dark stream. . . .

Is not this flight our human faring?

Is not this urge our human dream?

Thus I, frail vessel, am forbidden

To take the foreign road, and dip

To scoop a drop; the ways are hidden

Of alien streams I may not sip.

YAKOV POLONSKY

(1819-1898)

The routine of Polonsky's uneventful life was compounded of teaching, editorial work and long years of service in the censorship department. It is true that he traveled abroad and spent some years in the Caucasus, but this did not interrupt the even tenor of his ways.

He was a prolific fiction writer, yet it is as a poet that he lives in the memory of his compatriots. His poetry itself has been charged with being "lukewarm and neither cold nor hot." It lacks, it has been said, that cosmic nostalgia and civic consciousness which belong to Russian poetry. Indeed Polonsky's poetic effigy is rather unheroic and indistinct in outline. Yet he has the virtues of his defects. His work is distinguished by its homeliness. It keeps to the lighted circle of our familiar and familial life, and foregoes power and passion for intimacy and charm.

THE COSMIC FABRIC[1]

This vast web, of Nature's weaving,

Is God's garment, so 'tis said.

In that fabric I—a living,

I—a still unbroken thread.

And the threads run swiftly, never

Halting, yet if once they sever,

Seer or sage shall not suffice

Then the parted strands to splice.

For the Weaver so will veil them

That (let him who may bewail them)

None the ends shall ever find,

Nor one broken thread rebind.

Ceaselessly the threads are breaking,—

Short, ah short will be my span!

Meanwhile, at His fabric's making

Toils the cosmic Artisan,—

Curious patterns still designing,

Wave and crested hill defining,

Steppe and pasture, cloud and sky,

Wood and field of golden rye.

Though with care the wise may scan it,

Flawless since that Hand began it,

Smooth and fine with fair accord—

Shines the garment of the Lord!

[1]Tr. by Avrahm Yarmolinsky and Cecil Cowdrey.

SORROW'S MADNESS

When, clinging to your lidded coffin,

I saw you, love, on your last journey go,

No sobs my maddened heart could soften,

And I seemed dead, like you, below.

Yours was the grave men see so often:

Your small frame fitted snugly, so;

With leaden stupor blinded, I beheld it

Vanish, I heard the clods' soft blow.

My coffin was not thus—but spacious,

And gay with leaves and a blue pall in state.

And fastened to it glared the sun of mid-day:

A gilded, gawdy coffin-plate.

Your coffin disappeared beneath wet earth and gravel,

But mine—alas!—still glittered mockingly. . . .

An orphaned soul and widowed, I let my sad eyes travel

About me, my heart's heart, and I could see

How, buried deep in my resplendent coffin,

And bearing death within me, I would sue

For happiness now lost forever;

I knew my nothingness, my thirst for you.

I longed to break the spell of numbness—

Lay waste my living tomb, wrench back its bars,

To tear aside the graveclothes of the heavens,

To stamp upon the sun and scatter wide the stars,

And dash across this endless graveyard

Where dead worlds fill the graves,

To find your dwelling where no memories languish,

To Death's void galley chained like sullen slaves.

VLADIMIR SOLOVYOV

(1853-1900)

Coming from a family of scholars and churchmen, Solovyov was himself a mystic and visionary: an alien seed in an exorcised age. He was a cross between a Bohemian and a lay monk, whose asceticism only emphasized his powerfully erotic nature. A spirit dedicated to the creation of the greatest philosophical system which Russia has given to the world was fain to express itself also in poetry. His one slender volume of lyrics has the quality of soaring spirituality, and is generally engaged with a supersensuous reality, occasionally broken by irruptions of spasmodic comedy. It is largely centered about the concept of the Eternal Feminine, which also plays an important part in his grandiose religious system. He conceives it not as Aphrodite, but rather as Sophia: Divine Wisdom.

This feminine principle materialized itself for the mystic in a Dantesque experience. In a reminiscential poem written eight years before his death, he relates how, as a boy of nine, he first glimpsed his Eternal Mate. This was in Moscow; he next sees her in the reading-room of the British Museum thirteen years later, as he bends over volumes of abstruse mystical literature. She bids him follow her to Egypt. It is a biographic fact that the young Dozent traveled across the continent to Cairo, and went afoot into the desert, where he beheld his beatific vision for the last time.

"BELOW THE SULTRY STORM"

Below the sultry storm that seemed to lower,
An alien force, again I heard the call
Of my mysterious mate: the prisoned power
Of old dreams flared and flickered in its fall.

And with a cry of horror and of dolor—
As of an eagle in an iron vise—
My spirit shook its cage in quivering choler,
And tore the net, and issued to the skies.

And up behind the clouds, unswerving, bearing,—
Before the miracles—a flaming sea—
Within the shining sanctum briefly flaring,
It vanished into white infinity.

"WITH WAVERING FEET"

With wavering feet I walked where dawn-lit mists were
lying,

To find the shores of wonder and of mystery.

Dawn struggled with the final stars, frail dreams were flying,

While unto unknown gods my morning lips were crying

The prayers that my dream-imprisoned soul had whispered
me.

The noon is cold and candid, the road winds on severely,

And through an unknown land once more my journey lies.

The mist has lifted now, and the stark eye sees clearly

How hard the mountain-road that rises upward sheerly,

How distant looms the dream the prescient heart descries!

Yet onward with unfaltering feet I shall be going

Toward midnight, onward toward the shore of my desires,

Where on a mountain-height, new stars its glory showing,

My promised temple waits, with plinth and pillar glowing,

Beaten about with flame of white, triumphal fires.

N. MINSKY

(Pseudonym of Nikolai Vilenkin; born 1855)

The son of poor Jewish villagers, Minsky was, among other things, tutor, lawyer, and bank employee, before he emigrated to Paris in 1905, at the age of fifty, where he has lived as newspaper correspondent and littérateur ever since. He had previously lived abroad, and was abreast of European literary movements.

His ideological and poetic career has been no less kaleidoscopic. Beginning as a poet insistent upon civic virtues and art as criticism of life, within some ten years Minsky became the prophet of a-moralism, decadence, symbolism, and the champion of Bacchic beauty. Early in the twentieth century he joined with sophisticated Orthodox priests and lay God-seekers in founding a society for the promotion of a new religious consciousness, himself preaching a nebulously negative, mystic doctrine of "meonism," affectionately envisaging a new Nirvana.

The revolution of 1905 inspired his Muse briefly to Marxian hymns, and helped him to his Parisian exile. Here, in addition to his other work, he wrote a dramatic trilogy. Minsky had a weakness for manifestos, of which his poetry was not always a successful illustration. It is only his later work, with its increased technical skill, that achieves the bodying forth of his curious intellection.

FORCE

She lies, opening her teats, strong, swollen, wide,

And at her breasts, their equal gift bestowing,

Mad Nero and meek Buddha clutch, unknowing,

As clinging twins who suckle side by side.

She holds two vessels, whence, forever flowing,

The streams of Life and Death serenely glide.

She breathes—and wreaths of stars are lit, and bide,—

She breathes anew: they fly like sere leaves blowing.

She looks ahead with cold unseeing eyes;

She cares not though she bear or cause to perish;

The children whom she nurtures she will cherish,

But when she weans them, every claim denies.

Evil and Good gather them in thereafter

And play the cosmic game with idle laughter.

MY TEMPLE

Who rears a temple, rears two monuments:

His own and the destroyer's. They who build

Accept Herostratos' arbitraments:

And to the torch the chisel's work is willed.

Both will stand firm before posterity,

And equal glory Fame to each will lend.

But thou, my air-domed temple, shalt not be

Mocked by the vengeance of the general end.

On an abyss of ruin is thy lease,

Thou'rt in the furnace of negation fired;

In thee the hymns of solace shall not cease:

With sorrow winged, by calm despair inspired.

Thee, ¹egioned sufferings guard, in iron mail,

And in their vanguard Death, who shall prevail.

DMITRY MEREZHKOVSKY

(Born 1865)

Merezhkovsky had every opportunity of study and travel afforded the son of a comfortably circumstanced, bureaucratic family. He made his pilgrimage to the seats of the antique Mediterranean culture, and the Parthenon brought him, like Renan, to his knees. Yet this devout and learned Hellenist is much of a lay theologian. He has constructed a professedly mystical, but actually rationalistic religion, which dominates all his work. The synthesis of paganism and Christianity, of flesh and spirit, which is his religion of "the Third Testament," is the Procrustean bed of both his brilliant criticism and his vast historical novels. In the latter his method is chiefly that of an historical mosaicist. His trilogy is accessible to the English reader, as well as some of his critical work, notably a part of his remarkable study on Tolstoy and Dostoyevsky.

His prose forms the bulk of his writings. As a poet, Merezhkovsky was one of the initiators of the modernist movement, but he counts mainly as the champion of their poetics. His own lyrical work is largely ineffectual and imitative of men as curiously alien to him as Baudelaire, Poe, and Nietzsche. Against a background of melancholy pieces, expressing metaphysical ennui and cold intellection, one finds some poems informed with spiritual beauty and religious intensity.

A PRAYER

Cast prostrate, in mourning,

Wingless, self-scorning,

Grief in a gust

Flings us, dust upon dust.

We desire not, we dare not,

We believe not, we care not,

No wisdom has worth.

God, do thou dower us,

Kindle, empower us,

Give of thy mirth.

From the languor that clings

Give us wings! Give us wings!

Wings of thy Spirit.

THE TRUMPET CALL

Over earth awakes a whirring,

And a rustling, and a stirring,

Trumpet-voices fill the skies:

"Lo, they call us. Brothers, rise!"

"No. The darkness holds unshaken.

I will sleep, and not awaken.

Do not rouse me. Do not call.

Do not strike the coffin-wall."

"Now you dare not sleep. Resounding

Sternly, the last trump is sounding.

They are rising from the tomb.

As from the maternal womb

Of the opened earth forth-flinging,

From their graves the dead are springing."

"No, I cannot. All unuttered

My words died. My eyes are shuttered.

I shall not believe their lies.

I shall not, I cannot rise!"

Brother,—I am ashamed and shrinking,—

Dust, corruption,—rotting, stinking!"

"Brother, God has seen our prison.

All shall wake, and all be risen.

All shall yet be judged by Him.

Cherubim and seraphim

High the holy Throne are bearing!

Here our heavenly King is faring.

Brother, he must live who dies.

Glad or grieving, thou shalt rise."

THE CURSE OF LOVE

With heavy anguish, hopeless straining,

The bonds of love I would remove.

Oh, to be loosed from their enchaining!

Oh, freedom, only not to love!

The soul that shame and fear are scourging

Crawls through a mist of dust and blood.

From dust, great God, my spirit purging,

Oh, spare me from love's bitter flood!

Is pity's wall alone unshaken?

I pray to God, I cry in vain,

More weary, by all hope forsaken;

Resistless love grows great again.

There is no freedom, unforgiven,

We live as slaves, by life consumed;

We perish, tortured, bound and driven,

Promised to death, and to love—doomed.

FYODOR SOLOGUB

(Pseudonym of Fyodor Teternikov; born 1863)

In Sologub the sick fantast thumbed his nose at the respectable schoolmaster. One would expect neither in the son of a tailor and a peasant woman, who had grown up in the house where his widowed mother was a servant. For ten years after his graduation from Normal School the young man taught in the provinces, learning to know the Main Streets of Russia, which were to furnish the stuff of his prose. At the age of twenty-nine he transplanted himself to St. Petersburg, where his un-canny verse and short stories gave him the entrée to the modernists' circle. In 1907 he retired from pedagogy, and devoted himself entirely to literature. A few years later his complete works were published in twenty volumes, five of which were poetry, the remainder fiction and drama. He is a stay-at-home, and has remained one, the revolution notwithstanding.

If Sologub did not exist, it would be necessary to invent him. The decadent gesture, which was a pose or a purpose in others, is his natural attitude. He sees the universe as a ghastly menagerie in which the beasts have become wonted to their own stench. From this he escapes to a world of impossible imaginings, and fills his isolation with liturgies to his own ego, hymns to the devil, hosannahs to death. His unearthly world is fevered with fleshy lusts. In his lucid moments, however, he achieves the charm of a Blake-like innocence, and his hemlock is mixed with the honey of an enchanting music. His poetry is the core of his work. His prose is fantastic and Poeesque, yet in one work at least, notably "The Little Demon," he follows the Russian realistic tradition of revealing human nature's repugnant depths.

THE AMPHORA

In a gay jar upon his shoulder

The slave morosely carries wine.

His road is rough with bog and boulder,

And in the sky no starlights shine.

Into the dark with stabbing glances

He peers, his careful steps are slow,

Lest on his breast as he advances

The staining wine should overflow.

I bear my amphora of sorrow,

Long brimming with the wine it hides;

There poison for each waiting morrow

Ferments within the painted sides.

I follow secret ways and hidden

To guard the evil vessel, lest

A careless hand should pour unbidden

Its bitterness upon my breast.

THE DRAGON

Evil dragon in the zenith fiercely glowing,

Filaments of flame across the heavens throwing,

Singeing all the valley with a heat that scorches,—

From the deep, dark quiver I will pluck an arrow

Tipped with subtle poison that shall find thy marrow:

All too early flourish thy triumphal torches.

I shall draw my bow in valiant retribution,

I, executor of ruthless execution,

And thy groaning answer my glad ears shall cherish

As I speed the sudden doom long overhanging,

And the arrow whizzes with a brazen twanging.

Thou shalt fade, thou evil dragon, thou shalt perish.

"WHEN, HEAVING ON THE STORMY WATERS"

When, heaving on the stormy waters,

I felt my ship begin to sink,

I prayed, "Oh, Father Satan, save me,

Forgive me at death's utter brink!

"If you will save my soul embittered

From perishing before its hour,

The days to come, the nights that follow

I vow to vice, I pledge to power."

The Devil forthwith snatched and flung me

Into a boat; the sides were frail,

But on the bench the oars were lying

And in the bow an old gray sail.

And landward once again I carried

My outcast soul, bereft of kin,

Upon its sickly vicious sojourn

My body and its gift of sin.

And I am faithful, Father Satan,

Unto my evil hour's vow,

When from my drowning ship you saved me

And when I prayed you guide the prow.

To you descend my praises, Father,

No day from bitter blame exempt.

O'er worlds my blasphemy shall tower;

And I shall tempt—and I shall tempt.

"AUSTERE THE MUSIC OF MY SONGS"

Austere the music of my songs:

The echo of sad utterance fills them,

A bitter breath, far-wafted, chills them;

And is my back not bent to thongs?

The mists of day on darkness fall;

The vainly promised land I follow

Upon a road the shadows swallow;

The world rears round me like a wall.

At times from that far land the vain

Faint voice will sound like distant thunder.

Can long abeyance of a wonder

Obliterate the long bleak pain?

THE DEVIL'S SWINGS

Below a pine's rough shadow,

Where loud the river sings,

The hairy-handed devil

Pushes his devilish swings.

He swings, and gives a crow,

To and fro

To and fro

The boards creak, bending low,

The taut rope rubbing slow

Against the heavy boughs.

The board sways back, and bracing,

With a long creak swings wide,

The devil, still grimacing,

Guffaws and holds his side.

I tremble to let go;

To and fro

To and fro

I sway and cling, but no,

My languid glances grow

Fast where the devil tows.

Above the looming pine

The blue fiend's sniggers sting:

"You found the swings so fine,

Well, devil take you, swing!"

Below the shaggy pine

They squeak and whirl and sling:

"You found the swings so fine?

Well, devil take you, swing!"

The fiend will not release
The board that hangs too steep
Till I am thrust toward peace
By the dark hand's dread sweep.

Until the hemp turns round
Too long, and is worn free,
Until the broad black ground
Comes flying up to me.

Above the pine I'll fling
And bore into the mire.
Then swing, devil, swing—
Higher, higher, higher!

ZINAIDA HIPPIUS

(Mme. Dmitry Merezhkovsky; born 1869)

Poetry is not woman's work in Russia. Zinaida Hippius, the wife of Dmitry Merezhkovsky, is one of the few who carry it on. She has written a great deal of bad fiction, some partisan criticism, rather indifferent dramas, and her poetry is not un-exceptionable. Soon after her literary marriage she joined the Petersburg symbolists, and with her husband was one of the founders of the Religious Philosophical Society. A weakness for religious discussion and a theosophic bias have done much damage to both her prose and her verse. Her later poetry, however, is interesting as the expression of her difficult and distinctive personality. She has the quality of burning ice, hiding under contemptuous ennui her passion for the impossible. In any event, she is a virtuoso of verse, whose mastery of tone-color and metric pattern is wholly admirable.

She is at present engaged, together with her husband, in writing hymns of hate against the Bolsheviki, from the bitter security of the Diaspora.

"I SEEK FOR RHYTHMIC WHISPERINGS"

I seek for rhythmic whisperings
Where noises bandy—
For life I listen wistfully
In footless banter.

I cast wide nets and tentative
In lakes of sorrow.
I go toward final tenderness
By pathways sordid.

I look for dewdrops glistering
In falsehood's gardens.
I save truth's globules glistening,
From dust-heaps garnered.

I fain would fathom fortitude
Through years of wormwood—
And pierce the mortal fortalice,
Yet live, a worldling.

My cup, through ways impassable,

To bear, untainted;

By tenebrous bleak passages

To joy attaining.

PSYCHE

A shameless thing, of every vileness capable,

It is as drab as dust, as earthly dust.

I perish of a nearness inescapable;

Its fatal coils about my limbs are thrust.

A shaggy poulp, embracing me, and pricking me,

And as a serpent cold against my heart,

Its branching scales are poisoned arrows sticking me;

Worse than their bite: repulsion's horrid smart.

Oh, were its sting a veritable knife in me!

But it is flaccid, clumsy, still and numb.

Thus sluggishly sucking the very life in me,

A torpid dragon, dreadful, deaf, and dumb.

With stubborn rings it winds in mute obscurity

And clings caressingly, its purpose whole.

And this dead thing, this loathsome black impurity,

This horror that I shrink from—is my soul.

CREATION

Thou queen of all serenity,

Soul of my soul, most chaste,

I summon thee, divinity,

I summon thee, make haste!

But to the tryst thy offering

Shall not be brought alone.

My guilt will come, my suffering,

My sin will lift its moan.

Before thy heart insulted so,

In shame my head will sink;

And I, who once exulted so,

My humble tears shall drink.

Forgive me that diurnity

Is all my love could dower;

That not for all eternity,—

I made thee for an hour.

Alone my will hath kindled here

Thy being from the void.

And thou shalt soon have dwindled here,

By my sole will destroyed.

As I, thou shalt grow tremulous,

Till all my strength is gone,

To fall, of silence emulous,

Into oblivion.

KONSTANTIN BALMONT

(Born 1867)

Balmont revived the tradition of the wandering minstrel. He traveled more widely than the old-fashioned troubadour and also more comfortably. His journeys carried him to Mexico and Egypt, to India and the South Seas, and winds from these exotic lands blow through his songs. His stay abroad was somewhat of an exile, as certain political poems written in 1906 barred him from Russia. This was a recrudescence of youthful political ardor, which, in his student years, sent him to prison for a short time, but which burned itself out early. He returned home in 1913, where he remained through the war and the revolution, till in 1920 he shook the dust of communism from his feet

Of late years, his reputation, which was enormous about a decade ago, has been on the wane. Yet his place as a great poet and as the leader of Russian modernism is assured to him in the opinion of his compatriots. He brought to Russian literature a spontaneous lyricism and a didacticism of joy which, while emancipating poetry from its gloom and social bias, failed of intensity, imagery, and intellection. What impressed his public was his vociferous æstheticism and a prolific versatility in subject-matter. He has certainly contributed to the language by his rhythmic inventions. His range includes poems about the colors, children's verse, abstruse mythology, adaptations of Russian folk-songs and spells, hymns to the elements, and, above all, pure lyrics. He is a veritable Narcissus of the ink-pot, to use a bon-mot of Tyutchev's. The "Hymn to Fire" is given here, not for its quality, but solely as a typical example of Balmont's manner. He has done a rare service to Russian letters by translating the poetry of many languages, including the Scandinavian. He has practically made an anthology of English verse, and also gave to Russia a partial Whitman and a complete Shelley. Like Ezra Pound, he takes pleasure in flaunting an obscure linguistic erudition. His fecundity, one fears, has survived most of his other faculties.

"WITH MY FANCY I GRASPED"[1]

With my fancy I grasped at the vague shadows straying,

At the vague shadows straying where the daylight had fled;

I ascended a tower, and the stairway was swaying,

And the stairway was swaying underneath my light tread.

And the higher I climbed, ever clearer were rounded,

Ever clearer were rounded dreaming hilltops aglow;

And from Heaven to Earth twilight voices resounded,

Twilight voices resounded from above and below.

And the higher I rose, strange horizons defining,

Strange horizons defining, did the summits appear;

And my eyes as I looked were caressed by their shining,

Were caressed by their shining, their farewell, sad and clear.

Now the night had appeared; Earth in darkness lay dreaming,

Earth in darkness lay dreaming, like a slumbering star,

While the smoldering sun, his dim embers still gleaming,

His dim embers still gleaming, shone for me from afar.

I had learned to ensnare the vague shadows far straying,

The vague shadows far straying, where the daylight had fled;

Ever higher I rose, and the stairway was swaying,

And the stairway was swaying underneath my light tread.

[1] Tr. by Avrahm Yarmolinsky and Cecil Cowdrey.

CENTURIES OF CENTURIES WILL PASS

Long centuries of centuries will pass, unsighted
Millenniums as locusts in deathy clouds descend,
And in the muttering of centuries affrighted
The same enduring firmament will watch the end.
The dumb, dead firmament—that God will not
  remember,
Who breathes Eternity behind the farther skies,
Beyond the fading of the last star's last slow ember,
Beyond the utter threshold words may scrutinize.
Forever cold, that starry desert, clouds out-topping,
Is flung forth, alien to the end, on space,
When tearing comet-fires will crumble with it, dropping
As dumbly burning tears from a despairing face.

IN THE WHITE LAND

The candid psalm of Silence rises whitely burning,
The icy wastes are lit with sunset's radiant yearning.
The drowsy elements in yawning vistas freeze,

And voiceless are the argent Polar liturgies.

Above the sea of whiteness, crimson curtains falling;

No fields or forests here, clear crystal shines appalling.

White altars stretch beneath the changeless icy skies,

A prayer, not suppliant, a psalm, not voiced,—arise.

HYMN TO FIRE

1

Oh, fire who purgeth us

In fate-kindled strife,

Thy beauty ruleth us,

Shinig with life!

2

Still and meek in the glow of a taper in church,

But in riot—tumultuous-tongued,

Unmoved by wild prayers, multi-faced,

Shot with color in walls overthrown,

Mad with passion, and nimble and gay,—

So triumphantly beautiful

That my eyes are alight with thy joy

Though thou feed on my own,—

O fair Fire, all my dreams are devoted to thee!

3

Eternally changeful,

Thou art Protean-faced.

Thou art smokily crimson

In the bonfires' roar.

Thou art as a flower of terror with petals of flame,

A bright mane of radiant hair.

In the tremulous flame of a taper thou burn'st

First in blue, then in shuddering gold.

In the silence of midsummer lightnings thou wak'st,

Burning coldly in storm-burdened clouds,

Eerily livid and dark.

In the thunder that crashes, the chanting of rain,

Thou art writ in the lightning's brief hieroglyphs,

In a quick broken flash

Or a long mighty shaft,

Now a ball with a nimbus of air all aglow

Where the swift-running gold

Is with scarlet besprent.

Thou art in the crystal of stars, in the comets' strong
   urge.

Sun-sent, thou dost enter the chambers of plants

With the gift of a quickening warmth.

Thou workest, thou wakest the secret of sap:

Flaming up in a scarlet carnation,

Pale gold in the whispering corn,

Or carelessly flung in a lithe drunken vine.

> Thou art lying in wait:
>
> As a spark in the night
>
> So thou leapest elate.

Thou art still in thy flight.

Soon thy glow shall abate,

But alive thou art great,

Than thy beauty is nothing more strange or more bright.

4

I shall chant thy high praises forever!

O sudden, O subtle, O terrible Fire!

Thy work is the melting of metals;

By thy aid are they fashioned and forged:

The ponderous horse-shoes;

The resounding and bright-bladed scythes:

That mow and that reap,

That mow and that reap;

Many circlets for lily-white fingers,

For ring-bounded lives,

For ring-fettered years,

As with lips growing cold the word 'love'

We repeat.

Thou createst the tools and machines

That shake mountains and shatter and smite,

The tools that find deep-buried gold, the keenness of weapons that kill.

5

Unto thee, omnipresent and sovereign, my dreaming I vow.

I am even as thou.

Thou dost light, thou dost burn, thou dost strive,

Thou art 'live, thou art 'live!

Of old a winged dragon thou wert, to the altar didst glide

Thence to ravish the bride.

And a fiery guest, a consoler who warmed to the bone

The young wife left alone.

O brilliant, a burning, O biting, O fierce,

In thy flame all the colors arise.

Thou art crimson and yellow, thy gleaming doth pierce

With the glow of chameleon gold and the scarlet that lights

autumn skies.

Thou art as a diamond with facets that shine,

As the feline caress of soft eyes that are heady as wine,

As the wave in its ecstasy breaking, an emerald line.

Like the leaf's iridescence agleam with reiterant Springs

In the dewdrop that trembles and swings.

Like the green dream of fireflies kindled at night,

Like the will-o'-the-wisp in the haze,

Like the dark, scalloped clouds the grave evening has gilded
with light,

That have spread forth their mourning upon the dim face of
the smoldering days.

6

I remember, O Fire,

How thy flames once enkindled my flesh,

Among writhing witches caught close in thy flame-woven
mesh.

How, tortured for having beheld what is secret,

We were flung to the fire for the joy of our sabbath.

But to those who had seen what we saw

Yea, Fire was naught.

Ah, well I remember

The buildings ablaze where we burned

In the fires we lit, and smiled to behold the flames wind

About us, the faithful, among all the faithless and blind.

To the chanting of prayers, the frenzy of flame,

We sang thy hosannahs, oh strength-giving Fire:

I pledged love to thee from the pyre!

7

Oh, Fire, I know

That thy light with an ultimate splendor our being shall
  drench;

It shall flare up before eyes that Death fain would finally
  quench.

With swift knowledge it burns, and with joy heaven-high

At the vastness of vistas unfolding afar.

Who has summoned those visions to being? And why?

Who has rayed them in colors befitting a star?

Beyond life is the answer.

Oh thou heavenward heart of the element ever in flight,

On my twilight horizon, let Death, necromancer,

Shed perpetual light!

VALERY BRUSOV

(Born 1873)

Brusov's biography coincides with his bibliography. He has filled his life with the labors of a curious-minded poet and a sensitive erudite. In 1913, at the age of forty, he began publishing the complete edition of his works in twenty-five volumes. In addition to poetry, original and translated, it includes two novels, tales, dramas, and critical work. His tales and dramas have a timeless, abstract quality, a curious combination of the Wellsian and the Poe-esque. His two large novels are marvelous studies in the archæology of the soul, restoring as they do the psyche of the Roman decadence and of Germany's dying Middle Ages.

Before he came of age he fell under the spell of the French symbolists and his argosy began by sailing under their colors. His European years sharpened these sympathies. He tried to transplant the French *vers libre* into Russian soil, and among other things, an anthology of French lyrics of the nineteenth century bears witness to his Gallic apprenticeship. Indeed, he achieved a leading place among the Russian symbolists, becoming an editor of their Moscow organ (*Vesy: The Balance*). Yet although he adopted all the manners and mannerisms of the neo-romantic reaction, such as aversion to reality, violent eroticism and extreme individualism, by temperament Brusov is more of a Parnassian. His later work shows a gravitation toward a soberer and more objective conception of art. His craftsmanship is careful and conscious, whether he wanders down the ages, dedicating a line to every god, or traces the pattern of his own moods, or, like his master Verhaeren, finds a rhythm for the voices of the city. According to Gautier's precept, he works *"dans le bloc résistant."* He has an eye for imagery and an ear trained to complex orchestration.

The revolution has not exiled Brusov, and he is laboring to preserve the continuity of Russia's culture. In a literary capacity he holds an important Government post.

THE TRYST[1]

In the land of Ra the flaming, by the shores of Nile's slow
waters, where the roofs of Thebes were seen,

In the days of yore you loved me, as dark Isis loved

Osiris, sister, friend and worshiped queen!

And the pyramid its shadow on our evening trysts would
lean.

Oh, the mystery remember of our meeting in the temple,

in the aisle of granite, dim and straight,

And the hour when, lights extinguished, and the sacred

dances broken,—each to each was sudden mate;

Our caresses, burning whispers, ardors that we could not

sate.

In the splendor of the ball-room, clinging to me, white

and tender,—through Time's curtain rift in twain,

Did your ear not catch the anthems, mingling with the

crash of cymbals, and the people's answering refrain?

Did you not repeat in rapture that our love awoke again?

Once before, we knew existence, this our bliss is a

remembrance,

and our love—a memory;

Casting off its ancient ashes, flames again our hungry

passion, flames and kindles you and me,—

As of old, by Nile's slow waters, in the land beyond the sea.

[1] Tr. by Avrahm Yarmolinsky.

"RADIANT RANKS OF SERAPHIM"

Radiant ranks of seraphim

Stir the air about our bed.

With their windy wings and dim

Our hot cheeks are comforted.

Low the circling seraphs bend,

And we tremble and rejoice

At hosannas that ascend,

Winged with their unearthly voice.

Cloudy luminous faces hover,

And the wing-swept candles wane.

And our fiery breasts they cover

As with hidden holy rain.

BENEDICTION

Que tes mains soient bénies, car elles sont impures.

C H A R L E S
BAUDELAIRE.

The shining of your golden eyes I bless!
That broke my dark delirium with light.

The smile that wavers on your lips I bless!
It kindled me like wine, it rent my night.

The poison in your kisses hid, I bless!
All thoughts, all dreams are poisoned by your kiss.

The scythe that sings in your embrace I bless!
All my past years you have mown down with this.

The fire of your awful love I bless!
I wrapped its flame about me joyfully.

The darkness of your spirit, lo, I bless!
For that its wings were outstretched over me.

Blessed all you gave, blessed what your soul denies:
I bless you for the grief, the dread, the pain;

That after you I strove toward Paradise;
That here without its gates, I stand in vain.

INEVITABILITY

If you kept faith, or not, does it avail?

If I was faithful or unfaithful to you?

Our eyes that would look elsewhere flinch and fail,

Yet not my will has power to undo you.

Once more I tremble, so once more you pale,

As the forebodings of old pain break through you.

The moments pour with noise of torrents streaming:

Above us passion's lifted blade is gleaming.

Whoever made us, lips and lit eyes drinking

Of lips and eyes, be it or God or Fate,

Is it not one? Within the circle shrinking

We stand to hear the spell reverberate!

We bend with happiness and fear,—and sinking,

We fall: two anchors on the sea-floor grate.

Fancy, nor chance, nor passion overpowers

Us, whom the ineluctable devours.

THE FIERCE BIRDS

Kindling the air, fierce birds with feathers of fire,

Through the white portals of Paradise flamed like desire.

Virgin vistas reared, lit with quivering red,

And beyond seas were the trackless wanderers fled.

But on the pillars of marble, on the threshold were thrown

Crimson shadows incredible, sunk in the stone.

And, under the arch, in eternity's radiance hidden,

Angels exulted in fruits that are secret and sweet and forbidden.

EVENTIDE

The posters shout, their gorgeous motley blares,

The signboards' groaning fills the street,

And from the shops a shrill light sharply flares,

As cries of triumph mock defeat.

Behind the glimmering panes soft fabrics sleep,

And diamonds pour their poison daze,

Above massed coins the lottery numbers leap

Like northern lights ablaze.

The burning streets like long canals of light

Flow on—the city is alive.

It swarms to celebrate the dawn of night

Like some unloosed and monstrous hive.

The sky and all its sentient stars are hid

By scattered arc-lamps beaming blue.

And harlots jostle sages where they thrid

The dancers in a rippling queue.

Between the gay quadrilles that form and break,

Among the waltzers, clanking slide

The tramways, with blue lightnings in their wake;

Like sheaves of fire, the motors glide.

Shame, like a leader his bright baton wielding

To the rank music of the wheels,

Has fused the thousand-throated throng, that yielding

As one, a holy chorus peals:

"Dust, we enthrone thee; brief and radiant Dust,

Dancing the round, we glorify,

About electric altars where they thrust

Their spears into the empty sky."

Oh, cover thy pale feet!

SAINT SEBASTIAN[1]

On slow and smoky fire thou burn'st and art consuméd,

Oh, thou, my soul.

On slow and smoky fire thou burn'st and art consuméd,

With hidden dole.

Thou droopest like Sebastian, pierced with pointed arrows,

Harassed and spent,

Thou droopest like Sebastian, pierced with pointed arrows,

Thy flesh all rent.

Thy foes encircle thee and watch with gleeful laughter

And bended bow,

Thy foes encircle thee and watch with gleeful laughter

Thy torments slow.

The embers burn, and gentle is the arrow's stinging,

'Neath the evening sky,

The embers burn, and gentle is the arrow's stinging,

When the end draws nigh.

Why hastens not thy dream unto thy lips, now pallid

With deadly drouth?

Why hastens not thy dream unto thy lips, now pallid

To kiss thy mouth?

[1] Tr. by Avrahm Yarmolinsky.

THE COMING HUNS

"Trample their Paradise, Attila!"

—VYACHESLAV
IVANOV.

Where do you stray, heavy Huns,

Who weigh on the world like a cloud?

Far, under Asian suns,

Your cast-iron tread is loud.

Swoop down in a drunken horde

From your dark encampments, rise

In a tide of crimson poured

Over this land that dies.

O slaves of freedom, pitch

Your tent by the palace gate.

Plow deep, dig wide the ditch

Where the throne shone on your hate.

Heap books to build a fire!

Dance in their ruddy light.

Foul altar steps with mire:

You are children in our sight.

And we, the poets, the wise,

From the onslaught that darkens and raves,

Defending the torch you despise,

Shall hold it in deserts and caves.

Under the scattering storm,

The tempests that raven and tear,

What will the hazards of harm

From our long labor spare?

All that we only knew

Shall perish and sink and grow dim.

But you who shall slay me, you

I salute with hosanna and hymn.

IVAN BUNIN

(Born 1870)

When Bunin came to Petersburg at the age of twenty-five he brought with him memories of shabby manorial grandeur, of hack work in the provinces, and of a Tolstoyan influence that at one time persuaded him to become a cooper. The young man, meeting the modernists for the first time, dubbed them "sick boys with complete chaos in their heads." Bunin is himself a traditionalist in an age of iconoclasm, a realist in a neo-romantic generation, a sober lyricist solitary among his ecstatic fellows. His minor music has the simplicity and sincerity of a sorrowful Mozart. He celebrates the melancholy charm of vanishing things, never foreswearing his classic clarity. Yet there is a growing exotic strain in this poet of the Northern Russian landscape. He is a less vivid Leconte de Lisle, revivifying forgotten deities and filling his verse with Oriental color, fragrance and warmth. His nostalgia for the distant seems to grow by the travel upon which it feeds. Perhaps this intimacy with what is foreign gives his translations from Longfellow, Byron and Tennyson their remarkably rich quality.

When in 1909 Bunin was elected to the Academy of Sciences, this rare distinction was conferred upon him for his prose as much as for his poetry. Indeed the former is the part of his work which bulks largest. His prose *œuvre* consists of his black and bitter sketches of the Russian peasantry, naked studies in psychology, and tales in the manner of a diminutive Joseph Conrad. "The Gentleman from San Francisco," one of his most recent and impressive stories, is the only one available in English.

Bunin was one of the first to flee Soviet rule, eventually settling in Paris.

RUSSIAN SPRING

In the valley the birches are bored.

On the meadows, fog billows and weighs.

Sodden, with horse-dung floored,

The highroad blackens in haze.

Rich on the steppe's sleepy air,

The odor of freshly-baked bread.

Bent to their packs, slowly fare

Two beggars to look for a bed.

Round puddles gleam in the streets.

The fumes of the ovens stun.

Thawing, the bleak earthen seats

Smolder and steam in the sun.

By the corn-bin, dragging his chain,

The sheep-dog yawns on the sill.

Walls smoke with the charcoal stain.

The steppe is foggy and still.

The carefree cock will perform

Day-long for the sap-stirred earth.

In the fields it is drowsy and warm.

In the heart—indolent mirth.

A SONG

I'm a plain girl, whose hands are stained with earth.

He is a fisherman—he's gay and keen.

The far white sail is drowning in the firth.

Many the seas and rivers he has seen.

The women of the Bosphorus, they say,

Are good-looking . . . and I—I'm lean and black.

The white sail drowns far out beyond the bay.

It may be that he never will come back.

I shall wait on in good and evil weather.

If vainly, take my wage, go to the sea

And cast the ring and hope away together.

And my black braid will serve to strangle me.

THE GOD OF NOON

Black goats I herded with my sister; they

Grazed by red rocks; the grass rose stiff and stinging.

Warming their backs, stones to the foot-hills clinging

Slept dumbly on. And sheer blue shone the bay.

By the gnarled silver of an olive flinging

My drowsy limbs, in its dry shade I lay,—

He came—like a hot cobweb net, asway,

Or like a cloud of flies about me singing.

He bared my knees. Kindled my quiet feet.

The silver on my shirt his white fire burned.

His hot embrace is heavy, ah, and sweet.

He laid me on my back. The whole sky turned.

He tanned my naked bosom to the teat.

From him the cammomile's kind use I learned.

IN AN EMPTY HOUSE

From the walls the paper's blue is vanished,

The daguerreotypes, the ikons banished.

Only there the deepened blue appears

Where these hid it, hanging through the years.

From the heart the memory is perished,

Perished all that long ago it cherished!

Those remain, of whom death hides the face,

Leaving their yet unforgotten trace.

FLAX

She sits on tumulus Savoor, and stares,

Old woman Death, upon the crowded road.

Like a blue flame the small flax-flower flares

Thick through the meadows sowed.

And says old woman Death: "Hey, traveler!

Does any one want linen, linen fit

For funeral wear? A shroud, madam or sir,

I'll take cheap coin for it!"

And says serene Savoor: "Don't crow so loud!

Even the winding-sheet is dust, and cracks

And crumbles into earth, that from the shroud

May spring the sky-blue flax."

VYACHESLAV IVANOV

(Born 1866)

Ivanov's life was not one to "hurry to a sphere, and show, and end." Rather, its fruit slower grew, and later hung. He began to write at the age of thirty-seven, after having spent half as many years abroad as a student, and joined the ranks of the symbolists. He learned antiquity from "Mommsen, Athens and Rome," and modernity from Nietzsche and Dostoyevsky. A curious feature of Ivanov's thinking is a synthesis of Dionysos and Christ, which is characteristic of the Greek revival in Russia, and which is attested to in his profound treatise on "The Hellenic Religion of the Suffering God." His exquisite art feeds on the Dionysian grape, but this has a sacramental flavor, and strangely through the features of his Dionysos shows the effigy of a tragic Christ. To him religion is the very stuff of culture, and art a myth-making, and even a theurgic power. Unlike his older fellow-symbolists, he builds not upon individualism, but upon the principle of *sobornost*, or communal religious expression suggestive of Vachel Lindsay's creed. He has the mentality and the manner of a mystagogue and a pontiff.

Ivanov's poetry is caviar to the general. His Pegasus is caparisoned with abstruse erudition and weighed down with intricate thought. Yet a limpid, golden beauty triumphs over the shadows in many lyrics. These are cast in the pure Grecian mold, these burn with "Æ"'s spiritual flame, and these are the ordered ecstasies of a Francis Thompson. His latest poems are a cycle of Winter Sonnets—written in blockaded Petrograd in 1920—filled with the sadness of resignation to loss and change.

THE CATCH

Now the golden leafage is beggared.

Shining through the porches of autumn,

Shows the cool blue stillness of heaven.

Lo, the thin-trunked grove is transcended:

Carved in stone, a columned cathedral.

Smoke-scrolls wind about the frail friezes;

Flung above the doors is a curtain—

Open-work: like nets of God's fishers

That the catch has slipped through and broken,

Like thy tatters, sacred and lovely,

At the entrance of a white temple,

Oh thou golden mendicant music!

AUTUMN

The air is sad and still. A bright transparency!

Enskied a woman veiled in light invisibly

Upholds a balance high above the clear sun's pouring,

The instant's equipoise, serene and frail, adoring.

But each sere leaf that from the trees falls, separate,

And lays upon the golden scales its trembling weight

May force the balance Summer's plenty freighted

Down to the wintry regions soon to darkness fated.

FOUNTAIN

Clear the fountain waters glowing,

Living streams, the well-springs flowing,

Cold, in darkling woods, a spring.

In the shed, cool stillness streaming,

O'er the well, a candle gleaming

On Christ's crown its gilding flings.

In the Eden field—a bower,

And a fountain, and a flower.

Christ, star-voiced, the spirit stills:

"Come, before the well-spring stooping,

Of my quiet waters scooping,—

For the stintless bucket fills."

THE SEEKING OF SELF

Dying, the seed will discover the self it finds in the losing.

That is, oh, Nature, thy law! That is thy lesson, oh, Man!

Hearing dark music, the poet knoweth no rest; he abideth—

Purer and purer the sound, clearer the fore-uttered word.

COMPLAINT

Your soul, born deaf and blind, inhabits

Jungles of sunless reverie,

Where with the crash of trampled saplings

Wild droves of dark desires roam free.

A torch I kindled in the darkness

To lead you to my starry gate,

With seeds of light in shining handfuls

The furrows of your night to sate.

I stand amid the trackless stretches

And hail you in the wilderness;

But lost in dark and dreary caverns

My cry sinks silent, answerless.

NARCISSUS: A POMPEIIAN BRONZE

Beautiful boy, like a faun here in loneliness roaming,
who art thou?

Surely no child of the woods: thine is too prideful
a face.

Music that moves in thy gait, the wrought grace of
thy sumptuous sandal

Tell thou art son to the gods, or the high offspring
    of kings.

Poised, with thy listening limbs, thou hast followed
    the lips of the forest,

Harkening, bending thy head, fingering softly the
    sound.

Was it the piping of Pan or the amorous sighing of
    Echo?

Whisper of dryads, or words fluent-limbed naiads
    repeat?

Pressing thy thigh with thy arm, now the light
    shoulder-fleece like a garland

Thou hast entwined on thy wrist, thou, like Liæus
    at rest.

Wonderful, art thou in truth the gay Bacchus,
    Nysæan nymphs cherished,

Hunter, whom goddesses loved, naked and idle and
    young?

Or art thou haughty Narcissus, whom secret sweet
    harmonies guided,

Wandering, languid with sleep, drunken, alone with
    his dream?

Go, seek the summoning nymph, oh thou blind, not

yet knowing thy image,

Go thou, but dare not to bend over the slumbering
wave.

Oh, if thou art not Narcissus, yet seeing thy face in
the waters,—

Stranger, I tremble,—anew, thou a Narcissus shalt
be.

FUNERAL

Of funerals, the saddest

Is love's that dies unanswered.

The soul has two to bury:

The soul of the beloved

And its own other selfhood.

And a third enters, living,

The funeral flame that wraps them;

His wings a yoke has weighted:

Him the wise lips of lovers

Call in their kisses, Eros,

And gods: the Resurrector.

THE HOLY ROSE

The holy Rose her leaves will soon unfold.

The tender bud of dawn already lies

Reddening on the wide, transparent skies.

Love's star is a white sail the still seas hold.

Here, in the light-soaked space above the wold,

Through the descending dew the arches rise

Of the unseen cathedral, filled with cries

From the winged weavers threading it with gold.

Here on the hill, the cypress, in accord

With me, stands praying: a cowled eremite.

And on the roses' cheeks the tears fall light.

Upon my cell the patterned rays are poured.

And in the East, the purple vines bleed bright,

And seething, overflow. . . . Hosannah, Lord!

NOMADS OF BEAUTY

"You are artists, Nomads of Beauty."

—"Flamings."

For you—ancestral acres,

And, choked, the graveyard waits.

For us, the free forsakers,—

The camp that Beauty fates.

For us—the daily treason,

The tents we daily flee,

Mocked by each dawning season

Of our captivity.

Believe the dimmer distance,

All curtains: magic veils,

All Springtides' green persistence,

Whole heaven's vasty gales!

Oh, vagrant artists, shepherd

Your droves of dreams unbound;

And sow, although you jeopard

The soon-abandoned ground.

And from your open spaces
Rush down, a whirling horde,
Where slaves tamed to the traces
Adore their overlord.
Trample their Edens, plow them,
Oh, Attila, with scars.
And grow—to Beauty vow them—
Your steppe flowers like stars.

YURGIS BALTRUSHAITIS

(Born 1873)

Born into a peasant family of Lithuanian Catholics, this member of the symbolists' younger generation began by herding cows in his native village. He tutored his way through high school, and reached the University of Moscow, where he soon veered from science to letters. He became both a linguist and a traveler, going west as far as Chicago.

Although Baltrushaitis may be claimed by the Lithuanian as well as the Russian literature, this reticent poet does not often avail himself of either tongue. He carries on the philosophical tradition of Russian poetry. His disciplined and concentrated art moves on a plane of abstractions. His is a mystical austerity and a Buddhistic aloofness from things personal.

THE PENDULUM

When the dumb darkness most heavily clings,
Rhythmic and ruthless my pendulum swings.
Rustily creaking or whining dismay,
Urging each tarrying moment away.

Longing, it seems, for the days that are fled,
Down ancient stairways resounds someone's tread.
Heavy the footfall on flagstones unlit,—
Lower and lower and down to the pit.

Praying, it seems, for a long-vanished shore,
Dumbly the Helmsman with slow stubborn oar
Brokenly row's me, morosely alone,
Into my harbor, afar and unknown.

Evil the Ferryman, darkly he pounds;
Farther and farther, more muffled resounds,
Hostile and hopeless the long downward climb:
Cold, ineluctable footsteps of Time.

THE SURF

The day's wild ocean sings and thunders,
And beats against the fatal shore,
This breaker with dumb sorrow sunders,
And these like laughing victors roar,
Their sheen—the joy of vernal wonders,
Their sheen—vast winter's shining hoar.

In wrath triumphant forward-swinging,
The lifted billow calls, and fails,
A joyous giant, shouting, singing,
Its voice the voice of sounding gales,
Its glory in the sunlight flinging
Whose noonday glow it holds and hails.

Across the sea, now lightly foaming,
Another rears, that stirs the deep,
And floods the shore with silence, gloaming;
Morose and slow it seems to creep
Like one who drops, worn out with roaming,
From his bent back a fatal heap.

Each moment new, with changing power,

The surf is thundering, alone.

Now idle, now it seems to lower,

Hymning a Silence all unknown,

Like a dark heart asleep,—for hour

On hour in restless monotone.

MAXIMILIAN VOLOSHIN

(Born 1877)

Of the three confessed elements of voloshin's life: places, books, and men, places came first. Born in Kief, his early impressions were associated with the Crimea, the Hellenic promontory of the Scythian plain. At twenty-three he glimpsed the desert of central Asia. But in his own words he found "the fatherland of his spirit" on the Mediterranean littoral. And Paris was peak on which the climbing poet came to rest, finding there the lifting consciousness of rhythm and form. Books came second: Russian, of course, and later foreign books: the sophistry of France and the wisdom of immemorial India. Men Voloshin admits, came last. And so his acid bites into the plate most frequently to etch still life, or a landscape where the presence of God or man is a thing remembered.

By his own acknowledgment, he learnt the art of verse from Ivanov, Balmont and Hérédia. Whatever he may have derived from the Russian poets, it is clear that he shares Hérédia's precision and plastic perfection, his sonority and color. Voloshin's is a richly visual poetry. Indeed, he has earned his bread as a painter. Like Hérédia, he is a sonneteer of consummate skill. The sonnet from "Lunaria", given here, concludes a cycle of fifteen, which are so written that the last line of each forms the first line of the next the final sonnet being composed of the first lines of the preceding fourteen. And finally, it may be said of him, as it was of Hérédia, that this Parnassian is a modernist. Yet he has ever stood aloof from coteries, an aristocratic and solitary figure

Athough seemingly *dépaysé* and above the battle, Voloshin has quite recently written several poems of exasperated and retrograde patriotism, which, irrespective of their politics, are magnificent poetry.

CIMMERIAN TWILIGHT I

The evening light has soaked with ancient gold
And gall the yellow hills. Like tawny fur
Grass rises shaggy in a ruddy blur;
past fiery bushes metal waves unfold;
And enigmatic cliffs and boulders hold
Worn troughs that are the sea's chronologer.
In the winged twilight figures seem to stir:

A heavy paw, a jowl grins stark and bold,

Like swelling ribs the dubious hillocks show;

On what bent back, like wool, does savory grow ?

What brute, what titan, to this region cleaves?

The dark is strange . . . and yonder, space is clean.

And there the tired ocean, panting, heaves,

And rotting grasses breathe of iodine.

CIMMERIAN TWILIGHT II

Here stood a sacred forest. Here the messenger

Wing-footed went, his touch upon the dumb glades
   leaving . . .

Upon the site of cities, nor stones, nor ruins heaving:

Now on burnt slopes but sheep in scattered patches stir.

The mountain peaks: cut crowns! Across each bitten spur

The clear green twilight flows, mysteriously grieving.

By whose dim longing stung, what is my soul retrieving?

Who knows the road of gods? The dawns and dusks that
   blur?

In its sonorous caves the rubble, churned, is sounding;

Lifting its weighty crests, the troubled sea is pounding

Upon the sandy dunes, upon the ringing shore.

The heavy nights pass on in tears through starry
spaces . . .

The outcast gods command, whom men invoke no more,

And ineluctably they show dark, alien faces.

CIMMERIAN TWILIGHT III

Above dark, rippled waters rises in retreat

Earth's heavy mass: the spines and rocky crests defying

The tortured steep in torrents of red rubble lying—

A lifeless land, its mourning reaches at my feet.

Sad dreams and solemn dreams flow by me, bitter-sweet:

Earth ancient and obscure, whose echoing bays are
sighing,

Where in late twilight with a sadder beauty dying

The waves in waste hexameters billow and beat.

And where no roadways run upon the dark's still rivers,

Breathing an ancient mystery, the dim sail swells and
    quivers

With winds of tossed desire and seas that lift and fall.

An alien tremor takes my ship upon its going

Where destined roads of daring and retribution call.

And lamp-like in the sky the Seven Stars are glowing.

SONNET XV

(From the Sonnet-cycle "Lunaria")

Pure pearl of silence brooding on the sky,

Presider o'er conception, lamp of dreams,

Altar of nightly spells, of crystal gleams,

Queen of the waters where thou lov'st to lie,

With what desire, where the long waves sigh,

Through my dark crucifixions, toward thy beams,

Toward Dian, toward fierce Hecate, there streams

The vision yet unlived that shall not die.

How strange thy diamond delirium shines

In thy fair hollows, in thy joyless lines,

And in the flashing mica of thy seas.

In listless ether thou art horror's face,

Thou, longing's cry, whom icy gaolers freeze,

Thou, dead world's avid corpse, cast out on space.

STIGMATA

Whose the flying hands, about me shedding

Fire, and leading me on passionate ways?

No sonorous stones my feet are treading,

But where vatic waters fill the days.

Piercing through the spirit, sharp pilasters

Rise, and candle sting the dark like bees.

Oh, the hearts that bloom like crimson asters,

Petalled with gold-bladed ecstasies.

Now the evening on the temple flinging

Patterned, carven crimson, shines and mourns.

Oh, the pale brow to the altar clinging,

Stung anew with stinging scarlet thorns!

The whole soul, high vaults and portals glowing,

Fear like incense swathes with dim blue bands:

Ah, I know you, sacred corals, growing

On the pierced palms of these outstretched hands.

MIKHAIL KUZMIN

(Born 1877)

This sensitive and precious *décadent*, who flaunts his descent from French émigrés and Russian noblemen, delights in literary masquerading. He is in turn an eighteenth century dandy, a Byzantine romancer, a contemporary of Boccaccio, or a *fin de siècle* Alexandrian. His Alexandrian Songs imprison all the exquisite fatigues and refined perversions of a culture cynical about its own passing. The texture of his poetry shows the care and competence lavished by a belle upon her complexion. His lyrics have the perfumed fragility and piquant charm of Somov's paintings.

"NOW DRY THY EYES"

Now dry thy eyes, and shed no tears.

In heaven's straw-pale meadows veers

Aquarius, and earthward peers,

His emptied vessel overturning.

No storming snows, no clouds that creep

Across the sheer pure emerald steep,

Whence, thinly-drawn, a ray darts deep

As a keen lance with edges burning.

"NIGHT WAS DONE"

Night was done. We rose and after

Washing, dressing,—kissed with laughter,—

After all the sweet night knows.

Lilac breakfast cups were clinking

While we sat like brothers drinking

Tea,—and kept our dominoes.

And our dominoes smiled greeting,

And our eyes avoided meeting

With our dumb lips' secrecy.

"Faust" we sang, we played, denying

Night's strange memories, strangely dying,

As though night's twain were not we.

FROM "ALEXANDRIAN SONGS"

Dying is sweet

On the battle-field

In the hissing of arrows and spears,

When the trumpet sounds

And the sun of noon

Is shining,

Dying for country's glory

And hearing around you:

"Hero, farewell!"

Dying is sweet

For an old, venerable man

In the house

On the bed

Where your forebears were born,—where they died,

Surrounded by children

Grown men,

And hearing around you:

"Father, farewell!"

But sweeter,

Wiser,

Having spent the last penny,

Having sold the last mill

For a woman

Who the next day is forgotten,

Having come

From a gay promenade

To the sold, dismantled mansion

To sup,

And to read the tale of Apuleius:

The hundred and first reading,—

In the warm, fragrant bath,

Hearing no farewell,

To open your veins;

And through the long skylight

Must come the scent of stock-gilliflower;

Dawn must be glowing,

And flutes be heard from afar.

GEORGY CHULKOV

(Born 1879)

Chulkov has versified in the strained mode current ten years ago, and has written novels that are diluted Dostoyevsky. He shared the latter's Siberian experiences, in fact, being exiled for participation in student disturbances. He early began to theorize about the necessity for a return to a more sober and realistic art enriched by the modernistic adventures.

"PURPLE AUTUMN"

Purple Autumn unloosened her tresses and flung them
On the heavens and over the dew-heavy fields.
She came as a guest to the old, silent house,
Singeing the grasses with red;
Through the garden she moved,—
Up the balcony; scarcely she touched
The fragile old rails.

She pushed the door-panel softly,

Softly she entered the room,

Sprinkling the rugs with her sun-yellow dust,

Dropped a red leaf upon the piano . . .

Ever after that hour, we heard her unceasing, her tireless
rustling,

Rustle and stir and soft whisper.

And our hands suddenly met

With no new words, new and forever false.

As though we had hung a wreath of red roses

On a black, wrought-iron door

Leading into a vault

Where lay the rotting body

Of a beloved dream.

Autumnal days were upon us,

Days of inscrutable longing;

We were treading the stairs

Of autumnal passion.

In my heart a wound,

Like the lamp of an ikon,

Burned and would not be quenched.

The cup of autumnal poison

We pressed to our lips.

By the serpentine garden path Autumn had led us

To crepuscular lilies

Upon the pale, sand-humbled pond.

And over the lilied waters and in the roses of evening,

We loved, more superstitiously.

And through the dark night,

On the languorous bed,

At the feet of my love,

I loved death anew.

The minutes rang tinkling like crystals

At the brink of an autumn grave:

Autumn and Death drunkenly clinked their glasses.

I pressed my thirsty lips

To the feet the ikon-lamp burnished,

I drank the cup of love.

Burned by the fires of sins,

Stretched on the cross of lusts,

Shamed, being needlessly faithless,

I drank the cup of love.

In the hour of ineffable dalliance

I sensed the whisper

Of autumn pain, of autumn passion.

And kisses like keen needles

Burned and pierced,

Weaving a wreath of thorns.

ALEXANDER BLOK

(1880-1921)

Alexander Blok was educated at the University of St. Petersburg, of which his grandfather was the rector. He belongs to the second generation of symbolists, and his first volume, which appeared in 1905, savors strongly of Solovyov's spirituality. The upheaval which was shaking his country is ignored in this book, instinct with vague eschatological expectations and devoted to the Eternal Feminine. Yet here she wears the medieval aspect of the Lady Beautiful, and spirit in her is married to flesh. These songs, employing an easy symbolic cryptogram, mingle the prayers of the postulant with a rarefied sensuousness. This asserts itelf in the succeeding volumes. The white melody is muffled by the voices of earth. Blok flees monastic walls for the confusion of the thoroughfares. The skirts of the Lady Beautiful are defiled, and the poet is stretched upon the cross of passion, with the bitter conviction that he is "fated to love her in Heaven only to betray her on earth." Christ and Russia are the other hypostases of Blok's trinity, their Golgotha strangely at one with his own. Whether he is a maker of masques for monastic harlequins, or another Œdipus before the Russian sphinx, whether he writes children's verse, lyrical dramas of an elusive symbolism, or poems reminiscent of the earlier Yeats, he reveals a keen emotional intensity and an unfailing sensitiveness of technique.

It was given to this delicate and remote lyricist to produce the most significant poem of the proletarian revolution. This is his striking epic, called "The Twelve," which is known far beyond the confines of Russia, and is accessible in half a dozen languages.

"INTO CRIMSON DARK"

Into crimson dark thou goest,
Thy vast orbits mock the eye.
Small the echo that thou throwest,
Far, I hear thy footfalls die.

Art thou near?—too far for greeting?
Lost in topless altitudes?
Shall I wait a sudden meeting
Where sonorous stillness broods?

In the solitude resounding

Distant footsteps echo free.

Is it thou who flamest, bounding

Circles of infinity?

THE UNKNOWN WOMAN

I have foreknown Thee! Oh, I have foreknown Thee.
   Going,

The years have shown me Thy premonitory face.

Intolerably clear, the farthest sky is glowing.

I wait in silence Thy withheld and worshiped grace.

The farthest sky is glowing: white for Thy appearing.

Yet terror clings to me. Thy image will be strange.

And insolent suspicion will rouse upon Thy nearing.

The features long foreknown, beheld at last, will change.

How shall I then be fallen!—low, with no defender:

Dead dreams will conquer me; the glory, glimpsed, will
   change.

The farthest sky is glowing! Nearer looms the splendor!

Yet terror clings to me. Thy image will be strange.

THE LADY UNKNOWN

Of evenings hangs above the restaurant

A humid, wild and heavy air.

The Springtide spirit, brooding, pestilent,

Commands the drunken outcries there.

Far off, above the alley's mustiness,

Where bored gray summerhouses lie,

The baker's sign swings gold through dustiness,

And loud and shrill the children cry.

Beyond the city stroll the exquisites,

At every dusk and all the same:

Their derbies tilted back, the pretty wits

Are playing at the ancient game.

Upon the lake but feebly furious

Soft screams and creaking oar-locks sound.

And in the sky, blasé, incurious,

The moon beholds the earthly round.

And every evening, dazed and serious,
I watch the same procession pass;
In liquor, raw and yet mysterious,
One friend is mirrored in my glass.

Beside the scattered tables, somnolent
And dreary waiters stick around.
"In vino veritas!" shout violent
And red-eyed fools in liquor drowned.

And every evening, strange, immutable,
(Is it a dream no waking proves?)
As to a rendezvous inscrutable
A silken lady darkly moves.

She slowly passes by the drunken ones
And lonely by the window sits;
And from her robes, above the sunken ones,
A misty fainting perfume flits.

Her silks' resilience, and the tapering
Of her ringed fingers, and her plumes,

Stir vaguely like dim incense vaporing,
Deep ancient faiths their mystery illumes.

I try, held in this strange captivity,
To pierce the veil that darkling falls—
I see enchanted shores' declivity,
And an enchanted distance calls.

I guard dark secrets' tortuosities.
A sun is given me to hold.
An acrid wine finds out the sinuosities
That in my soul were locked of old.

And in my brain the soft slow flittering
Of ostrich feathers waves once more;
And fathomless the azure glittering
Where two eyes blossom on the shore.

My soul holds fast its treasure renitent,
The key is safe and solely mine.
Ah, you are right, drunken impenitent!
I also know: truth lies in wine.

"A LITTLE BLACK MAN"

A little black man ran through the city.

He extinguished the lanterns, climbing the stairs.

Slow and white, dawn was approaching,

With the strange little man climbing the stairs.

Where quiet, soft shadows brooded over the town,

Where the yellow strips of the lanterns were sleeping,

Morning twilight upon the steps lay down,

Into the curtains, into the door-shadows creeping.

Oh, how poor is the city with dawn at her windows
   lying!

Crouching outside, the little black man is crying.

RUSSIA

To sin, unshamed, to lose, unthinking,

The count of careless nights and days,

And then, while the head aches with drinking,

Steal to God's house, with eyes that glaze;

Thrice to bow down to earth, and seven

Times cross oneself beside the door,

With the hot brow, in hope of heaven,

Touching the spittle-covered floor;

With a brass farthing's gift dismissing

The offering, the holy Name

To mutter with loose lips, in kissing

The ancient, kiss-worn icon-frame;

And coming home, then, to be tricking

Some wretch out of the same small coin,

And with an angry hiccup, kicking

A lean cur in his trembling groin;

And where the icon's flame is quaking

Drink tea, and reckon loss and gain,

From the fat chest of drawers taking

The coupons wet with spittle-stain;

And sunk in feather-beds to smother

In slumber, such as bears may know,

Dearer to me than every other

Are you, my Russia, even so.

"WHEN MOUNTAIN ASH"

When mountain-ash in clusters reddens,

Its leafage wet and stained with rust,

When through my palm the nail that deadens

By bony hands is shrewdly thrust,

When leaden-rippling rivers freeze me,

As on the wet gray height I toss,

While my austere-faced country sees me

Where I am swinging on the cross,

Then through my bloody agonizing

My staring eyes, with tears grown stiff,

Shall see on the broad river rising

Christ moving toward me in a skiff.

And in his eyes the same hopes biding,

And the same rags from him will trail,

His garment piteously hiding

The palm pierced with the final nail.

Christ! Saddened are the native reaches.

The cross tugs at my failing might.

Thy skiff—will it achieve these beaches,

And land here at my cruciate height?

THE SCYTHIANS

> "Pan-Mongolism—though   the
> word is strange,
>
> My ear acclaims its gongs."
>
> —VLADIMIR
> SOLOVYOV.

You are the millions, we are multitude

And multitude and multitude.

Come, fight! Yea, we are Scythians,

Yea, Asians, a squint-eyed, greedy brood.

For you: the centuries; for us: one hour.

Like slaves, obeying and abhorred,

We were the shield between the breeds

Of Europe and the raging Mongol horde.

For centuries your ancient hammers forged

And drowned the thunder of far hates.

You heard like wild fantastic tales

Old Lisbon's and Messina's sudden fates.

Yea, so to love as our hot blood can love

Long since you ceased to love; the taste

You have forgotten, of a love

That burns like fire and like the fire lays waste.

All things we love: clear numbers' burning chill,

The ecstasies that secret bloom.

All things we know: the Gallic light

And the parturient Germanic gloom.

And we remember all: Parisian hells,

The breath of Venice's lagoons,

Far fragrance of green lemon groves,

And dim Cologne's cathedral-splintered moons.

And flesh we love, its color and its taste,

Its deathy odor, heavy, raw.

And is it our guilt if your bones

May crack beneath our powerful supple paw?

It is our wont to seize wild colts at play:

They rear and impotently shake

Wild manes—we crush their mighty croups.

And shrewish women slaves we tame—or break.

Come unto us, from the black ways of war,

Come to our peaceful arms and rest.

Comrades, while it is not too late,

Sheathe the old sword. May brotherhood be blest.

If not, we have not anything to lose.

We also know old perfidies.

By sick descendants you will be

Accursed for centuries and centuries.

To welcome pretty Europe, we shall spread

And scatter in the tangled space

Of our wide thickets. We shall turn

To you our alien Asiatic face.

For centuries your eyes were toward the East.

Our pearls you hoarded in your chests,

And mockingly you bode the day

When you could aim your cannon at our breasts.

The time has come! Disaster beats its wings.

With every day the insults grow.

The hour will strike, and without ruth

Your proud and powerless Paestums be laid low.

Oh pause, old world, while life still beats in you.

Oh weary one, oh worn, oh wise!

Halt here, as once did Œdipus

Before the Sphinx's enigmatic eyes.

Yea, Russia is a Sphinx. Exulting, grieving,

And sweating blood, she cannot sate

Her eyes that gaze and gaze and gaze

At you with stone-lipped love for you, and hate.

Go, all of you, to Ural fastnesses,

We clear the battle-ground for war;

Cold Number shaping guns of steel

Where the fierce Mongol hordes in frenzy pour.

But we, we shall no longer be your shield.

But, careless of the battle-cries,

Shall watch the deadly duel seethe,

Aloof, with indurate and narrow eyes.

We shall not move when the ferocious Hun
Despoils the corpse and leaves it bare,
Burns towns, herds cattle in the church,
And smell of white flesh roasting fills the air.

For the last time, old world, we bid you come,
Feast brotherly within our walls.
To share our peace and glowing toil
Once only the barbarian lyre calls.

FROM "THE TWELVE"

9

The city's roar is far away,
Black silence broods on Neva's brink.
No more police! We can be gay,
Comrades, without a drop to drink.

A boorzhooy, a lonely mourner,

His nose tucked in his ragged fur,

Stands lost and idle on the corner,

Tagged by a cringing, mangy cur.

The boorzhooy like a hungry mongrel:

A silent question stands and begs;

The old world like a kinless mongrel

Stands there, its tail between its legs.

ANDREY BELY

(Pseudonym of Boris Bugayev; born 1880)

Reared in a professorial atmosphere, in which science was
the major element, Boris Bugayev, better known under his
pseudonym of Andrey Bely, has lived a double life of artist
and analyst. The artist was engrossed in problems of form.
He created an interesting, experimental genre which he called
"symphony," with cadenced prose, verbal instrumentation and
musical development of themes. The analyst, on his part, used
mathematic formulæ on the poet's fine frenzy, inaugurating
a science of rhythmics, at least for the Russians. Yet Bely is
no æsthete, but a mystic, who gropes toward the light of
Christ, "the timeless taper," and who lives by the uncertain
hope of the ineffable coming. The metaphysical conflict is
constantly invading the field of his poetic endeavor, until his
lyrics become the battle-cries of his spiritual tourneys. He is
responsible for more theorizing about symbolism than any
one else, but characteristically enough, he erects this nebula
into a *Weltanschauung* and almost into an ethics.

His poetry is rarefied and difficult. Its delicate imagery

is but an overtone of a resonant spiritual note. His poems have an esoteric quality which is also evidenced in his two famous novels, "The Silver Dove" and "Petersburg." Through both moves a curious counterpoint of the apocalyptic and the homely, muffled by theosophic speculation.

The proletarian revolution elicited from Bely a cycle of poems, suggestively entitled "Christ Is Risen!" Herein he envisions Russia, of which he once despaired, as the new Nazareth. Quite recently he completed the first part of a mosnumental epic planned for ten volumes.

MESSENGERS

In fields hopeless and dumb

Droops the pale-bladed grain;

It is dozing and numb

Amid dreams that are vain. . . .

With a high sudden hum

The field tosses its mane:

"Unto us Christ is come!"

The wild news shakes the plain.

Like a wind-beaten drum

Shouts the quivering grain.

The bells ring soft and slow,
There is clamor and pain
In the church, and a low
Voice is lifted again
That reiterates: "Woe!"
To the poor folk and plain
Are brought candles aglow:
"Christ is coming again!"
But with voices of woe
They file doorward, in pain.

EUTHANASIA

The shining and ponderous goblet
I empty: the earth drops below me,
All things sink away,—I am treading
Cold space—the vast void—the dim ether.
But distant, in ancient space looming,
My glimmering goblet: the Sun.

I look—far below me are lying

The rivers, the forests, the valleys,

Estranged in the vanishing distance.

A cloud, blowing fog on my eyelids,

Trails gossamer gold in its going.

The flickering landscape is burning

Its last: mid-day stars newly-kindled

Look into my soul, sparkling: "Welcome,"

With radiance silently streaming:

"The end of long wanderings, brother,

Lies here, in your motherland, welcome!"

Slow hour upon hour in procession,

Slow centuries, smiling, pass onward.

In ancient space proudly I lift it,

My glimmering goblet: the Sun.

"YOU SIT ON THE BED THERE"

(Opening poem of the "Funeral Mass" cycle)

"You sit on the bed there

In the sunset's full crimson,

Pillows crumpled,

Looking distracted,—what

Troubles you?"

        "Oh, swept by

        Transparent

        Gold cataracts,

        The fir-tree tops

        Loom athwart the sky's blue."

"Orphaned, alone, I shall

Languish,

Through summery

Twilights and Winter nights.

There are new flights, but

Try them I dare not.

Oh, do not die!"

> "Oh, above the pines
>
> I float off into æther seas.
>
> Who, there, what, there,
>
> Swathes the sky with whitenesses,
>
> As with vestments of silver?"

VICTOR HOFMAN

(1882-1911)

Hofman has to his credit some short stories and two books of lyrics, the second of which appeared two years before his suicide in Paris.

"STILL WAS THE EVENING"

Still was the evening of the ball,

The summer ball, with dancers wending

Where ancient linden shadows fall

Upon the river steeply bending;

Where in the trees the breezes breathe

And willows droop like drowsy dreamers;

Where it seemed beautiful to wreathe

The lanterns and the colored streamers.

A languorous waltz of slow retreatings,

A waltz that singing hardly sounded;

And many faces, many meetings,

Soft clouds like women's shoulders rounded.

The river looked a sculptured stream,

Serenely the whole heaven holding,—

A fluent and enchanted dream

Of joyous miracles unfolding.

A crimson mantle, golden-bright,

Upon the clouds the sun was flinging;

The dream-swept waltz was drowned in light,

And calling through the dusk and singing.

A languorous waltz beside the river,

And many meetings, many faces,

And near cheeks' warmth, and lovely quiver

Where eyelash with curved eyelash laces.

VASILY BASHKIN

(*c.* **1880-1909**)

In his prose Bashkin chronicled the career of Russia's radical intellectuals, and as a poet he acted the part of a tame Tirtæus in the camp of the revolution. He was cut off by tuberculosis early in life.

"UPON THE BLACK BROW OF A CLIFF"

Upon the black brow of a cliff where no life ever stirred
Alighted strong, hoary-winged eagles, grave bird upon bird.

They whetted their claws on the stones, sitting massive and grum,
And loudly they called on their lately-fledged comrades to come.

Slow-measured and heavy the beat of their wings on the skies,

Assuageless the rage that tempestuous burned in their eyes.

And each newly-come they acclaimed with the pride of the peer:

"Hail, comrade! Delay not! The days we have longed for are near."

SERGEY GORODETZKY

(1884-1921)

This rather uneven and sometimes slovenly poet worshiped at many shrines. He was a lyric myth-maker with Ivanov, a symbolist with Blok, an advocate of several fashionable doctrines, including mystical anarchy and mystical realism. At the head of the "Guild of Poets" which was formed shortly before the war, Gorodetzky attacked symbolism with Johnsonian zeal in the name of the "Acmeist" faith in realities. The poet became a jingo patriot when Russia entered the war, and later was as vociferously allied to the Bolsheviks as he had been to his Czar. His best work is informed with spirited spontaneity. The poetic restoration of the obscure Russian paganism, and a few lyrics carrying the dancing lilt of the folksong, form his chief contribution.

YARILA[1]

First to sharpen the ax-flint they bent,

On the green they had gathered, unpent,

They had gathered beneath the green tent.

There where whitens a pale tree-trunk, naked,

There where whitens a pale linden trunk.

By the linden tree, by the young linden,

By the linden tree, by the young linden,

The linden trunk

White and naked.

At the fore, shaggy, lean, hoar of head,

Moves the wizard, as old as his runes;

He has lived over two thousand moons.

And the ax he inhumed.

From the far lakes he loomed

Long ago.

It is his: at the trunk

The first blow.

And two priestesses in their tenth Spring

To the old one they bring.

In their eyes

Terror lies.

Like the trunk their young bodies are bright,

Their wan white

Hath she only, the tender young linden.

One he took, one he led,

To the trunk roughly wed,

A white bride.

And the ax rose and hissed—

And a voice was upraised

And then died.

Thus the first blow was dealt to the trunk.

Others followed him, others upraised

That age-old bloody ax,

That keen flint-bladed ax:

The flesh once,

The tree twice

Fiercely cleaving.

And the trunk reddened fast

And it took on a face.

Lo,—this notch—is a nose,

This—an eye, for the nonce.

The flesh once,

The trunk twice—

Till all reddened the rise

And the grass crimsoned deep.

On the sod

In the red stains there lies

A new god.

[1] The Russian Dionysos.

THE BIRCH TREE

Upon an amber day I loved you first,

    When, summoned by the radiant azure,

    From every grateful twig there burst

    Sweet indolence in dripping measure.

Your whitely shining body gleamed as white

    As heady foam on lakes unfolding,

    Gay laughing Lel[1] drew out the bright

    Black hair, its beauty lightly holding.

Himself, the god Yarila[2] crowned your hair

    With garlands green in gorgeous pleasure,

    And flung it, plaited, to the air:

    Green glory tossed upon the azure.

[1] The Russian Pan.

[2] The Russian Dionysos.

ANNA AKHMATOVA

Anna Akhmatova was at one time identified with the Acmeist group, which represented a reaction against symbolism. The work of this talented lyricist is notable for its classic tendency and an insistence on purely personal themes. Her tenuous verse delights in a sophisticated simplicity. The first of her four slender volumes appeared in 1912.

"LIKE A WHITE STONE"

Like a white stone deep in a draw-well lying,
As hard and clear, a memory lies in me.
I cannot strive nor have I heart for striving:
It is such pain and yet such ecstasy.

It seems to me that someone looking closely
Into my eyes would see it, patent, pale.
And, seeing, would grow sadder and more thoughtful
Than one who listens to a bitter tale.

The ancient gods changed men to things, but left them

A consciousness that smoldered endlessly,

That splendid sorrows might endure forever.

And you are changed into a memory.

CONFESSION

From my poor sins I am set free.

In lilac dusk the taper smolders;

The dark stole's rigid drapery

Conceals a massive head and shoulders.

"Talitha kumi": Is it He

Once more? How fast the heart is beating . . .

A touch: a hand moves absently

The customary cross repeating.

"BROAD GOLD, THE EVENING"

Broad gold, the evening colors glow,

The April air is cool and tender.

You should have come ten years ago,

And yet in welcome I surrender.

Come here, sit closer in our nook,

And turn gay eyes at what my nurses

Might never glimpse: the blue-bound book

That holds my awkward childish verses.

Forgive me that I did not look

Sunward with joy, but dwelt with sorrow,

Forgive me all whom I mistook

For you, oblivious of the morrow.

PRAYER

Give me comfortless seasons of sickness,

Visitations of wrath and of wrong

On my house; Lord, take child and companion,

And destroy the sweet power of song.

Thus I pray at each matins, each vespers,

After these many wearying days,

That the storm-cloud which broods over Russia

May be changed to a nimbus ablaze.

IGOR SEVERYANIN

(Pseud. of Igor Lotarev)

The story goes that at the beginning of his poetic career Severyanin took his constitutional on the Nevsky Prospekt wearing a yellow shirtwaist, with green roses painted on his cheeks. He enjoys the distinction of having founded the ego-futurist group in Petrograd, which opposed the cubo-futurist group in Moscow. He later betrayed the coterie, but remained faithful to its canons of sound against sense. His insistence on neologisms and words created *ex nihilo* has produced a style which is becoming a poetic idiom. Yet a genuine musical quality saves some of his intolerably clownish and vacuous verse. His first book, "The Thunder-Seething Cup," was published in 1913 and ran into seven editions in two years, and he has now some ten volumes to his credit. His poetry recitals have diverted both Czarist and Bolshevist Russia.

AND IT PASSED BY THE SEA-SHORE

Poeza Mignonette

And it passed by the sea-shore, where the foam-laces flower,

Where the city barouches only rarely are seen. . . .

There the queen played her Chopin in the high palace tower,

And there, listening to Chopin, the young page loved the queen.

And what passed there was simple, and what passed there was charming:

The fair page cut the pomegranate as red as her dreams,

Then the queen gave him half thereof, with graces disarming,

She outwearied and loved him in sonata-sweet themes.

Then she gave herself stormily, till night shut her lashes.

Till the sunset the queen lay, there she slept as a slave. . . .

And it passed by the sea-shore where the turquoise wave washes,

Where sonatas are singing and where foam frets the wave.

A RUSSIAN SONG

Lace and roses in the forest morning shine,
Shrewdly the small spider climbs his cobweb line.

Dews are diamonding and blooming faery-bright.
What a golden air! What beauty! Oh, what light!

It is good to wander through the dawn-shot rye,
Good to see a bird, a toad, a dragon-fly;

Hear the sleepy crowing of the noisy cock,
And to laugh at echo, and to hear her mock.

Ah, I love in vain my morning voice to hurl,
Ah, off in the birches, but to glimpse a girl,

Glimpse, and leaning on the tangled fence, to chase
Dawn's unwilling shadows from her morning face.

Ah, to wake her from her half-surrendered sleep,
Tell her of my new-sprung dreams, that lift and leap,

Hug her trembling breasts that press against my heart,

Stir the morning in her, hear its pulses start.

SPRING APPLE TREE

Aquarelle

An apple-tree in Spring shakes me,—to see it grow,

Its branches whitely weighted with unmelting snow.

So might a hunch-backed girl stand, beautiful and
dumb,

As trembling, the tree stands, and strikes my genius
numb. . . .

It looks into the wide, pale shallows, mirror-clear,

Seeking to shed the dews that stain it like a tear;

And stilled with horror, groans like a rude, rusty cart,

Seeing the dismal hunch mocked by the pool's bright art.

When steely sleep alights upon the silent lake

For the bent apple-tree, as for a sick girl's sake,

I come to offer tenderness the boughs would miss,

I press upon the petal-perfumed tree a kiss.

189

Then trustingly, with tears, the tree confides her care

To me, and brushes with a touch my back-blown hair.

Her boughs encircle me, her little twigs enlace,

And I lift up my lips to kiss her flowering face.

NIKOLAI KLUYEV

This sophisticated folk-poet, a peasant by birth, began to write just before the outbreak of the war, when he brought out three volumes of verse within two years. His mastery of his medium has developed steadily. His imagery, vivid and concrete, derives from two sources: the routine of rural life and Christian symbolism. Kluyev hailed the social revolution, and Russia as its messiah. His most recent work, "The Izba Songs", has a quality of deep and original homeliness.

A NORTHERN POEM[1]

Sunset dreams on fir-tree cones,
 Green—the hedge, and brown—the field;
Mossy rifts in weathered stones
 Meekly vernal waters yield.

Oh, look up the wooded steep—
 God has touched it with his palm;
Piously wild berries weep,

Listening to the grassy psalm.

And I feel no fleshly tie;
      And my heart's a springing mead.
Come, ye pilgrims white and shy,
      Peck the early wheaten seed.

Tender evening twilight searches
      Cottage windows, gabled byres,
And the leaves of slender birches
      Glimmer soft as wedding fires.

[1] Tr. by Avrahm Yarmolinsky.

AN IZBA SONG

The stove is orphaned now; the old housewife has died,

The trivet tells the pot with tears; their talk is harried.

Behind the pane two trustful magpies, side by side,

Chirp: "May is near, today the finches will be married,

Smith Woodpecker with busy knocking has stripped his

throat,

The mole—the sullen miner—creeps sunward, meekly leaving

His tunneled, dark estate to bugs without a groat.

The cranes are homing now, the sparrow, pert and thieving,

Has heard the jackdaw blurt the secret of her egg."

The tangled mop awaits the bucket, limp and tired.

She thinks the unwashed porch for spuming suds must beg.

How gay would be the splash of water, how desired

A windowful of sunray tow,—an endless fairy-tale . . . .

Behind the stove the house-sprite gabbles, quick and clever,

Of the new tenant's stillness within the churchyard's pale,

Of crosses listening to things nameless forever,

Of how the dark church-entrance lulls the linger dream.

The house-sprite gabbles on above the bleak hour's starkness.

The peasant-hut is scowling; pewter eye agleam,

The lonely window stares out at the thaw and darkness.

LUBOV STOLITZA

This young woman poet exhibits a charm which is insistently and delightfully feminine.

A LENTEN ONE

Noon in golden thaw is garbed with glory,

Midnight's wrap of silver snows is hoary.

Pink the buds among the aspen's ashes

Where the diamond hoar-frost softly flashes.

My kind cat has furtively departed,

But the swallow has returned, high-hearted.

Winter grief no more our dumb lips locking,

But upon the heart Spring grief is knocking.

And at noon we weep, our bosoms crossing,

Midnight sees us in hot slumber tossing:

Quiet lips, knees pressed as though in prayer,

But our shadowed eyes are our betrayer.

SERGI YESENIN

One of the latest comers, Yesenin is also one of the most gifted of the younger Russian poets. His first book was published in 1916. He is a member of a group which has come into being during the revolution and which calls itself *"imazhinisty"* (imagists). Like Kluyev, he came from the masses, and, like him, operates with the intimate details of the peasant's life and faith. Whatever his political and literary associations, he is a poet *dei gratia*.

"UPON GREEN HILLS"

Upon green hills wild droves of horses blow
The golden bloom off of the days that go.

From the high hillocks to the blue-ing bay
Falls the sheer pitch of heavy manes that sway.

They toss their heads above the still lagoon
Caught with a silver bridle by the moon.

Snorting in fear of their own shadow, they,
To screen it with their manes, await the day.

"HOPES PAINTED BY THE AUTUMN COLD"

Hopes, painted by the autumn cold, are shining,
My steady horse plods on, like quiet fate,
His moist dun lip is catching at the lining
When the coat, flapping, flutters and falls straight.

On a far road the unseen traces, leading
Neither to rest nor battle, lure and fade;
The golden heel of day will flash, receding,
And labors in the chest of years be laid.

.

"IN THE CLEAR COLD"

In the clear cold the dales grow blue and tremble;
The iron hoofs beat sharply, knock on knock.
The faded grasses in wide skirts assemble

Flung copper where the wind-blown branches rock.

From empty straths, a slender arch ascending:
Fog curls upon the air and, moss-wise, grows,
And evening, low above the wan streams bending,
In their white waters washes his blue toes.

TRANSFIGURATION: III

Eh, Russians,

Fowlers of the universe.

You who trailed heaven with the net of dawn,

Lift your trumpets!

Beneath the plow of storm

The dumb earth roars.

Golden-tusked, the colter breaks

The cliffs.

A new sower

Roams the fields.

New seeds

He casts into the furrows.

A guest of light drives toward us

In a coach.

Across the clouds

A mare races.

The breech-band on the mare:

The blue;

The bells on the breech-band:

The stars.

Z. SHISHOVA

This is one of the more gifted of the woman poets in the youngest choir.

"HOW STRANGE, OH, GOD"

How strange, oh, God, as in sleep's euthanasia,
Thy earth today.
Behind the window, each like an acacia,
The poplars sway.

From my small muff my hand withdrawing slightly,
I find it dry.
And from my furs, as though May touched them lightly,
Faint perfumes fly.

And through the night dark troubled dreams are rearing:
They choke and cling.
How shall I then forbear at last from fearing,
Oh, God, thy Spring?

PIOTR ORESHIN

Oreshin belongs to the poetic progeny of the Revolution.

NOT BY HANDS CREATED

1

Fall on your face,

Drop

Mug-forward into the swamps.

With your old were-wolf's eye,

Cataract-blinded,

Look

What a blade I am!

2

Carrot-haired

Big-browed dawns,

And the darkness of forests,

Rye,

And the sheaves behind the village,—

My body.

3

Long ears,

Tufted with red hair,

Wag

Like asses' ears

Through the heavens!

4

Two

Convulsed eyes—

Two

Oceans resting in me,

And thick

Bulbous lashes

Burning green

On my cheek-bones.

5

My stone mouth

Is stretched with song

From east to west.

6

Legs

And hoofs

Kicked skyward

And

The claw

On my hairy paw

Blazes.

7

Gorged

And motionless,

Like a bull,

I have squatted, rock-fast,

In a long shirt

Of sunsets,

And I sit now

Sprawled out

On the fat hill of the universe.

8

Dark forests

Grow

On my hairy belly,

And in the stony fir-trees

Gray wolves,

In cope and coif,

Having lit a taper,

Serve

The mass.

9

Eternal,

Not by hands created,

I roll my eyes heavily

As roll the mill-stones

Of the blue

Mills

Of heaven.

10

Slowly

I chew the cud of gray clouds,

And

Think

Of perishing brothers

With my wise

Cheerful belly.

11

Through closed lids

I see

Between my legs new rivers

Heave

New ground

Upon golden

Crests.

12

Listening to the earth,

I spit

With out-thrust, lower lip,

And lo!

Rains

Pour with the sound of spears

And, clinking,

Pierce the earth.

13

Eternal,

Not by hands created,

With the spirit of Life-giving Spring

I sweep

The tilled field,

And

On the naked knees of the universe

I pour

The blue waters

Of My Eternal Triumph.

Hosannah in the highest!

ANATOLY MARIENHOF

This young poet belongs to the Imagist coterie. His verse is interesting for its sophisticated technique and its angular ruggedness. The title of the second poem given here refers to the month when the Soviets assumed power.

"SAVAGE, NOMAD HORDES"

Savage, nomad hordes
Of Asia
Poured fire out of the vats!
Razin's execution is avenged,
And Pugachov's pain
Whose beard was torn away.
Hooves
Have broken
The scruff of the earth,
Cold with centuries,

And the supernal sky, like a stocking

With a hole in its heel

Has been taken out of the laundry-trough

Wholly clean.

OCTOBER

We trample filial obedience,

We have gone and sat down saucily,

Keeping our hats on,

Our feet on the table.

You don't like us, since we guffaw with blood,

Since we don't wash rags washed millions of times,

Since we suddenly dared,

Ear-splittingly, to bark: Wow!

Yes, sir, the spine

Is as straight as a telephone pole,

Not my spine only, but the spines of all Russians,

For centuries hunched.

Who makes a louder noise on earth now than we?

You say: Bedlam—

No milestones—no stakes—

Straight to the devil——. On the church porch our red
cancan is glorious.

What, you don't believe? Here are hordes,

Droves of clouds at men's beck and call,

And the sky like a woman's cloak,

And no eyelash of sun.

Jesus is on the cross again, and Barabbas

We escort, mealy-mouthed, down the Tverskoi
Prospekt. . . .

Who will interrupt, who? The gallop of Scythian horses?

Violins bowing the Marseillaise?

Has it ever before been heard of, that the forger

Of steel bracelets for the globe

Should smoke his rotten tobacco as importantly

As the officer used to clink his stirrups?

You ask—And then?

And then dancing centuries.

We shall knock at all doors

And no one will say: Goddamyou, get out!

We! We! We are everywhere:

Before the footlights, in the center of the stage,

Not softy lyricists,

But flaming buffoons.

Pile rubbish, all the rubbish in a heap,

And like Savonarola, to the sound of hymns,

Into the fire with it. . . . Whom should we fear?

When the mundiculi of puny souls have become—
worlds.

Every day of ours is a new chapter in the Bible.

Every page will be great to thousands of generations.

We are those about whom they will say:

The lucky ones lived in 1917.

And you are still shouting: They perish!

You are still whimpering lavishly.

Dunderheads!

Isn't yesterday crushed, like a dove

By a motor

Emerging madly from the garage?

www.ingramcontent.com/pod-product-compliance
Lightning Source LLC
Chambersburg PA
CBHW022126080426

42734CB00006B/248